Staying Open

An Essential Guide for Managers of Licensed Premises

Michael Watson & Deon van Niekerk

Copyright © 2020 Michael Watson & Deon van Niekerk

All rights reserved.

ISBN: 9798699920280

No part of this publication may be reproduced, stored in a retrieval system, or transmitted in any form or by any means, electronic, mechanical, photocopying, recording, scanning, or otherwise, without the prior written permission of the author.

Limit of Liability/Disclaimer of Warranty: This publication is designed to provide accurate and authoritative information in regard to the subject matter covered. While the authors have used their best efforts in preparing this book, they make no representations or warranties with respect to the accuracy or completeness of the contents of this book and specifically disclaim any implied warranties of merchantability or fitness for a particular purpose. No warranty may be created or extended by sales representatives or written sales materials. The advice and strategies contained herein may not be suitable for your situation. You should consult with a professional when appropriate. The authors shall not be liable for any loss of profit or any other commercial damages, including but not limited to special, incidental, consequential, personal, or other damages.

CONTENTS

	Foreword	1
	About the Authors	3
	Introduction	7

Section 1: Background — 11

1	Outline of the Licensing Act	12
2	The Importance of the Four Licensing Objectives	20
3	The Problems Operators Face	25

Section 2: Prevention — 29

4	Terms of Entry	30
5	Young People	39
6	Search/Seizure	45
7	Preventing and Dealing with Intoxication	49
8	Drugs Awareness	58
9	Prevention & Intervention	65
10	Door Supervisors	69
11	Events & Private Hire	82
12	Management of Outside Area & Dispersal	84
13	CCTV, Body Worn Cameras (BWC) & Identity Scanners	88
14	Record Keeping	94

Section 3: If the Worst Happens: Reactive Measures — 98

15	Guest Welfare	99
16	Ejections	110
17	Dealing with Serious Incidents	117

18	Crime Scene Preservation	120
19	Incident Reporting and Investigating	124
	Section 4: Consequences	132
20	Remedial Action and Closure Powers	133
	Section 5: Dealing with the Statutory Authorities	137
21	Successfully Dealing with Inspections	138
	Conclusion	144
	Appendix 1: BETTER Compliance Licensing Heat Map	145
	Appendix 2: Preventing Positional Asphyxiation	146
	Useful Links	151

FOREWORD

Now that you are in possession of "Staying Open – An Essential Guide for Managers of Licensed Premises" you may consider yourself among the fortunate. It will repay its reading many times over.

A premises licence permitting the sale of alcohol, provision of regulated entertainment or late night refreshment is a precious asset. It is, however, a fragile instrument. With regulators increasingly baring their teeth, and the licensed sector being very much in their crosshairs, this publication is as timely as it is welcome. To be forewarned is to be forearmed.

Michael Watson and Deon van Niekerk have distilled their extensive knowledge, personal insights, and long experience of licensing issues into a short, engaging and highly readable book. It not only points out the potential pitfalls for licensees but also provides the reader with the practical tools needed to avoid them. Prevention is always better than cure.

The fact that the authors' vast experience comes from both the regulator and licensee sides of the licensing world greatly enhances their ability to give practical advice and guidance.

Too many licensees are losing their licences and facing prosecutions for myriad reasons ranging from breaches of licence conditions to allegations that the premises is associated with crime and disorder, causing a public nuisance, or jeopardising public safety or the prevention of harm to children licensing objective. The authors highlight all the licensing risks and clearly set out real-world methods to help avoid them from de-railing your business.

The writers are a formidable force batting for the licensed sector and if, despite the invaluable guidance within this book, you find yourself needing licensing help, you will find that they are fine people to have on your side.

Gary Grant
Barrister
Francis Taylor Building, Inner Temple, London
www.ftbchambers.co.uk

Gary Grant is one of the UK's leading licensing barristers. He is top-ranked in both of the major independent legal directories (Legal 500: "the go-to counsel for licensing matters" and Chambers Guide: "Star Individual; just brilliant, determined to win and a very eloquent advocate, one of the best of the best"). He practises from the leading licensing set at Francis Taylor Building in the Inner Temple, London. He is Vice-Chairman of the Institute of Licensing and a Consultant Editor of Paterson's 2018-2021 ("the bible of licensing law"). Further information at www.licensingbarrister.com.

ABOUT THE AUTHORS

Deon van Niekerk

In 2001 I opened my first night club, Cherry Jam, in West London to critical acclaim. Artists such as Mark Ronson and Chase and Status were among the resident DJs and the Libertines did their first ever concert there.

I opened my second club, Neighbourhood, nearby after purchasing Subterania from Vince Power in 2004. The club had a stellar line up of residents including Love Box with Groove Armada, Dimitri from Paris, and Felix Da Housecat. It was what I had always wanted to do.

What I didn't realise was that by opening busy clubs on the edge of residential areas, I had stepped into a battle zone.

The clubs rattled the cages of some powerful and influential local residents who called in the cavalry to try and get the venues closed down. From the moment I opened, the statutory authorities laid siege.

Police, police licensing, council licensing enforcement, environmental health officers, noise abatement teams, and custom and excise would come down night after night for inspections. It was overwhelming.

Despite searching for help, I struggled to find anyone with the skills and experience I needed. So I turned to my licensing lawyer for help who had put himself forward as an expert. He began advising me on what I should be doing but it soon became clear he didn't understand the intricacies of running a club and, when pressed, admitted he had rarely set foot in a nightclub before.

I was on my own. I set about learning to bridge gaps between resident associations, various areas of law enforcement, and how to engage productively with various stakeholders. I joined police steering groups and various council improvement groups. I learned what was important and how best to manage extremely fluid and volatile situations.

I also realised there was a huge disconnect between the expectations of authorities and what my managers and staff knew.

This disconnect is what results in venues being closed, onerous conditions being added to the premises licences, and people losing their businesses.

It was around this time that a friend, Allana McCabe, introduced me to Michael Watson.

With his licensing knowledge and strong background in enforcement in Clubs and Vice (CO14) and Islington Council, he knew exactly what was required to keep my business compliant with the Licensing Act and how, as a business owner, I could protect my key asset — the premises licence, along with my substantial financial investment.

With a background in DJing in clubs, Michael also had an excellent understanding of the importance of atmosphere and guest experience in running a successful venue.

We started working together in 2005 and developed our BETTER Compliance system to empower the venue staff with the knowledge and tools to do their jobs without jeopardising my licence and instead, protecting it.

Michael was hugely sympathetic and knowledgeable about the sector and swiftly became a key member of our core team.

Having almost lost my club due to conflicting requirements and a sense of complete overwhelm, I know firsthand what it's like to see your dream falling apart with no idea how to control it. Michael and I live and breathe the hospitality industry and we are passionate about helping owners stay open and overcome the issues they face.

We believe that licensing compliance doesn't have to be boring or a drain on resources and morale. Compliance, when done well, enhances everyone's experience — both guests and staff alike. We deliver our service with energy and passion to invigorate and inspire the staff we work with.

Michael Watson

After working as a licensing officer with both the Metropolitan Police and the London Borough of Islington, I have been delivering licensing solutions for over twenty years to some of London's leading nightclubs, bars, and restaurants.

I have experienced the frustrations of bureaucracy, shifting regulations, and the headaches of licensing firsthand. I can spot structural compliance issues and can demonstrate the benefits to a business when they work closely with the right authorities in the right way.

Shortly before the Licensing Act 2003 came into effect in 2005, I knew that I wanted to move into the commercial sector and work as a consultant. I could clearly see that there was a gap between operators and the authorities. I also knew most licensees wanted to do the right thing but were extremely busy, overwhelmed with laws and regulations, and had a lack of awareness of best practice in achieving compliance.

In many instances, licensing lawyers were filling that gap in reaction to issues. But a proactive approach was required, and it was not necessarily a lawyer's role to give practical advice on operational matters relating to compliance.

Don't get me wrong, this is not a criticism of licensing lawyers. As a consultant, I enjoy working with many of the best licensing lawyers in the country, often in a supporting role providing positive evidence at hearings and working with their clients to develop operations manuals, policies, and procedures.

I am the first person to recommend seeking expert legal advice and representation if the situation demands it. However, I could see that operators needed advice and guidance on the ground from someone who had observed and conducted a detailed audit of their operation whilst they were trading at 2am, and who knew exactly how a licensed premises was inspected by the authorities and what their expectations would be. Even better, by someone who understood the business and the problems faced by licensed premises.

STAYING OPEN

Aside from my professional career as a licensing officer, I had also spent much of the 1990s and 2000s DJing around London. I was keenly interested in live music so was very familiar with London's nightlife. I had a great deal of sympathy for late licensed premises and the issues they faced.

The catalyst for my transition from officer to consultant was being introduced to Deon van Niekerk in 2005. I was finishing my final year at Birmingham University studying licensing law part-time. The new Licensing Act was coming into effect at the end of that year and the time was right for something life-changing.

A mutual friend introduced me to Deon saying that they thought we would get on well, and they were right; we hit it off immediately both on a personal a professional level. I was impressed by his relentless creativity and entrepreneurial spirit.

We shared many of the same opinions on the hospitality industry; we both understood that most licensees wanted to do the right thing but were overwhelmed with laws and regulations that they didn't comprehend or just had a lack of awareness of. We are also both natural problem solvers and enjoy finding creative solutions to challenges.

Our licensing consultancy was an immediate success and very unusual in the sense that we were not 'finger waggers' finding fault; our ethos is identifying vulnerability and providing realistic and effective solutions. Our mission is to provide peace of mind and protect the client's key asset – their premises licence. Our backgrounds in hospitality meant we approached issues with empathy, knowing the strategies had to be affordable and not prohibitive to business.

As consultants, we realised our reach was limited by time and geography. We were fortunate enough to be working with some of the best premises in London's nightlife, but we knew that our services and expertise would be invaluable to a much wider section of the industry. We knew that the service needed to be affordable and accessible to all and so the business evolved into the BETTER Compliance system.

I am proud to say that BETTER Compliance does exactly what it says on the label: provide all the tools, policies and procedures, and support an operator needs to ensure better compliance.

STAYING OPEN

This book is born from our combined experience and distilled from all the elements of our BETTER Compliance system.

INTRODUCTION

"Success is a journey, not a destination. It requires constant effort, vigilance and re-evaluation."
- Mark Twain

One of the biggest challenges facing managers and owners in the hospitality and leisure sector is the sheer volume of legal compliance and know-how needed to navigate the complex laws.

When it comes to licensing, each statutory authority you deal with — whether it's someone from council or police licensing enforcement, an environmental health officer, the Health and Safety Executive, the Information Commissioner, or the fire safety officer — expects you to be an expert in their particular field.

You are expected to know what you are talking about and what to do to comply with the law governing their area. Ignorance of the law, as everyone knows, is no excuse.

The price to pay for getting this aspect of the business wrong can be devastating. Changes of personnel are often insisted upon and reviews can be brought against your premises licence. Closures can follow reviews, adverse changes made to your licence; licensees can be prosecuted, receive unlimited fines, and even be jailed.

Staying Open provides the solution of staying ahead of the game. In this book, we share our experience to provide practical, easy-to-use advice combined with succinct information, step-by-step guides, and useful flowcharts on what you need to do in each of the assessed areas.

Using our BETTER Compliance framework, you will fully understand the legal requirements and how to easily implement compliance measures into your business. It will give you a clear understanding of the issues you face and simple solutions to solve and prevent problems when it comes to licensing compliance.

As a result of our BETTER Compliance framework, we've helped staff become confident in dealing with the authorities, seeing interactions as an opportunity to build rapport and impress rather than something to be nervous of. We've put preventative measures in place and come up with innovative solutions. We've won the respect of the authorities who even started to push back on the residents due to their groundless complaints.

Over 15 years, we have helped hundreds of premises save and protect their licences and, in many cases, enhance them using our framework. We now work closely with most of London's leading clubs and bars on a monthly basis. Our clients include The Box, Tape London, Cirque Le Soir, Hilton Park Lane, Mahiki, Swingers (Crazy Golf), Maxwell's Restaurants, and many more.

The drawback to this approach is that due to the hands-on nature of the work, it's an expensive service and only a handful of clubs found it accessible. It always sat uncomfortably with us that many people who needed us the most could not afford it. We did pro bono work where we could but there is a limit to how much you can do for free.

So, to make our service accessible to everyone, we created an online platform that takes small hospitality business owners through our six-step BETTER Compliance system. The platform allows us to deliver peace of mind to many more businesses across the UK at a fraction of the cost. It consists of the entire BETTER framework with added webinars, newsletters, workshops, and advice lines. It even includes our very popular RASPFLO™ (Responsible Alcohol Service and Promoting Four Licensing Objectives) online course.

After years of success in the business of licensing compliance and regulation, we know what works. Our accelerator system is a tried and trusted methodology designed to do one thing – ensure BETTER Compliance.

The BETTER Compliance System

For the best results, we suggest joining our BETTER Compliance system along with implementing the insights in this book. Here is what you can expect as a member:

Step 1: Buy In
There needs to be demonstrated dedication to compliance and promoting the four licensing objectives with a clear commitment from the leadership team. Licensing compliance needs to be at the centre of what you do.

Step 2: Evaluate
A comprehensive self-audit that generates a strategic action plan you can use to assess the vulnerabilities and gaps in the company's current licensing regime and put the focus on what you need to do.

Step 3: Tune-In Tools Installed
Having identified the critical success factors required, next we implement the right tools including policies and procedures, checklists, due diligence record keeping, plus an incident reporting management system.

Step 4: Training
Targeted and ongoing training giving your staff the knowledge they need to succeed, making implementing new systems clear and straightforward. Our unique online RASPFLO™ (Responsible Alcohol Service and Promoting the Four Licensing Objectives) course for serving staff and managers ensures your workforce is trained to the highest standard.

Step 5: Effective Management and Monitoring
Following training, you will consistently measure the success and effectiveness of operational procedures and aim to build a body of positive due diligence evidence for the premises. Audits serve as an excellent management tool giving you confidence that your business is compliant and act as an early warning alert if issues are identified. Your managers will become used to the inspection process and be able to handle any statutory authority visits confidently and effectively.

Step 6: Re-Evaluate
Finally, you will be given systems to constantly re-evaluate your compliance regime, considering shifting circumstances, changes in legislation, best practice, and current guidance from the authorities. We are on hand throughout the process to give you advice and support as

required.

Staying Open is a companion guide for the BETTER Compliance system. But this book is also of huge value to managers of licensed premises in its own right. Reading it will give you a greater understanding of your responsibilities and, if used in conjunction with the BETTER Compliance system, will help you achieve a much higher level of compliance through best practice.

SECTION 1
Background

CHAPTER 1
Outline of The Licensing Act

"You have to learn the rules of the game, and then you have to play better than anyone else."
- Albert Einstein

Any business, organisation or individual who wants to sell or supply alcohol or provide other licensable activities in England and Wales must have a licence or other authorisation from a licensing authority, usually the local council.

Your licence is your business' key asset, so you must always behave in a way that protects the premises licence. There are severe penalties for failing to uphold the licensing objectives including fines, being jailed, or the licence being suspended or revoked which could result in the business having to close down and everyone losing their jobs.

Premises Licences

Any premises which is used for licensable activities will generally require a premises licence. Licensable activities include:
- Selling alcohol
- Serving hot food and drinks between 11pm and 5am

You may also need a licence if you provide the following types of entertainment:
- Theatrical performance
- Showing a film
- Indoor sporting event
- Boxing or wrestling (indoor or outdoor)
- Live music

- Recorded music
- Performance of dance

Licences are granted by the local council which operates as the licensing authority. Licences will state the times that you may operate and will have mandatory conditions specific to your premises.

Premises licences can be granted to allow licensable activities to take place up to 24 hours, 7 days a week and may allow more than one type of licensable activity. With regards to late night refreshment, a licence is only needed between 23:00 hours and 05:00 hours.

The licence itself is issued in two parts:
- The premises licence – includes conditions and a plan. A certified, original copy should be kept available and in a safe place for inspecting officers.
- The premises licence summary — similar to the premises licence but without the conditions and plan. This must be on prominent display at the premises.

Once granted, a licence generally runs indefinitely unless the licence holder surrenders it, becomes insolvent, dies, or becomes mentally incapable. If this happens, the licence may be reinstated under certain circumstances, but you must act within 28 days if you wish to transfer the licence. A licence may also be suspended or revoked by the licensing authority.

An annual fee is payable for the licence and is determined by the rateable value of the business. This fee must be paid on time to avoid the licence being suspended.

Why are Premises Licensed?

There is a general perception that the provision of licensable activities can lead to crime and disorder, public nuisance, risk to public safety, and harm to children. Licensing is a way of controlling these activities and ensuring only professionally managed premises are allowed to operate.

The Licensing Act 2003 outlines the requirements for permission to obtain a licence and states four key objectives that underpin all decisions and processes concerning licensing matters:
- Prevention of crime and disorder

- Public safety
- Prevention of public nuisance
- Protection of children from harm

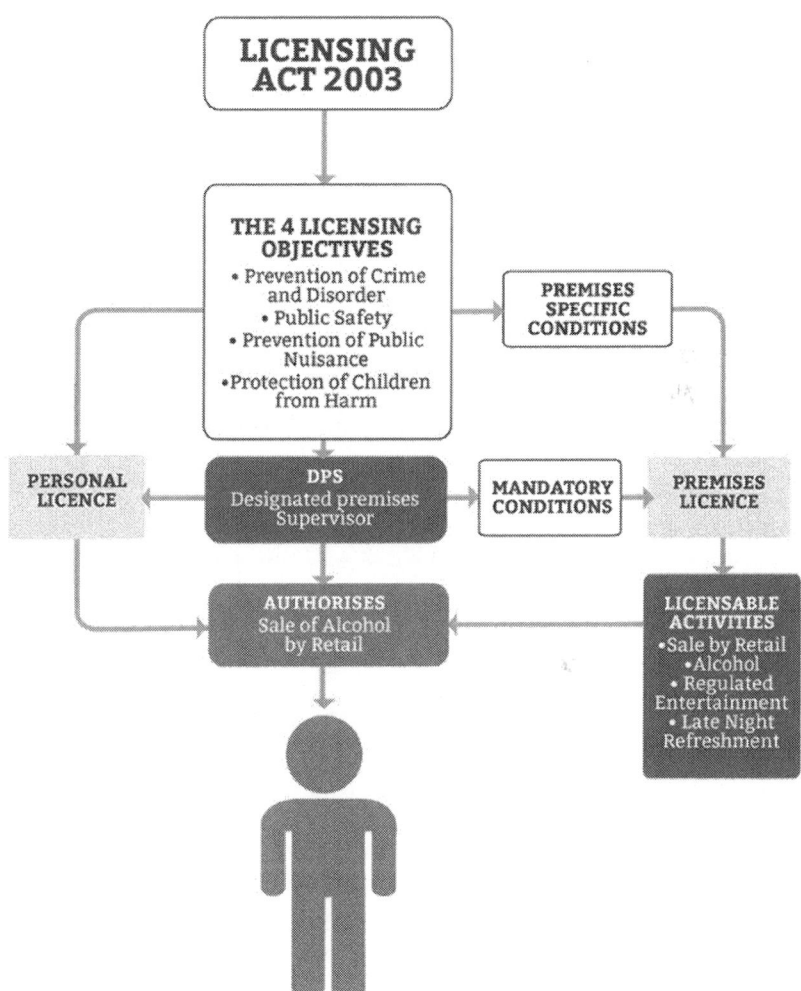

Revoking a Premises Licence

It is a criminal offence to operate outside the terms and conditions of the licence. If prosecuted, you can be fined or worse. A licence may also be subject to a review application at any stage. Responsible authorities or

any other person can apply for a review. For example:
- A resident or resident's group
- Another business
- Ward councillor
- Police
- Fire brigade
- Environmental health

The review must be based on reasonable grounds (that is, not frivolous, vexatious, or repetitive) and must relate to at least one of the four licensing objectives.

There is a 28-day period where the application for review is publicly advertised on the premises, at the council offices, and on the council's website. During this time, other parties may make representation. After this time, the matter is considered at a public hearing by the council's licensing committee.

A review of the licence is a very serious matter and the licensing committee may change the conditions. For example, they may reduce the operating times, impose extra conditions, suspend the licence for up to three months, remove the Designated Premises Supervisor (DPS), or revoke the licence.

Personal Licences

A personal licence allows the holder to sell alcohol as well as authorise 'others' to sell alcohol at a premises which has a premises licence. A personal licence is 'portable' in that the holder can authorise sales of alcohol at more than one premises, however, it is not transferable between individuals.

Personal licences are granted by the local authority or council where the individual lives when they first apply. This council will remain the personal licence holder's 'home authority'. The holder of the licence must always inform their home authority council of any changes to their name or address.

The personal licence is comprised of a photocard and paper certificate – both parts constitute the licence.

There are several regulations regarding a personal licence:

- Any premises licensed to sell alcohol will need at least one personal licence holder.
- Any premises licensed to sell alcohol will need one Designated Premises Supervisor (DPS) named on the licence. The DPS must hold a valid personal licence.
- A personal licence holder does not legally need to be on-site at all times alcohol is being sold unless it is a specific condition of the licence. However, it is best practice.
- A personal licence holder must produce their personal licence if requested by an authorised officer.

Mandatory Conditions

The same mandatory conditions appear on all premises licences which authorise the supply of alcohol:

- All sales of alcohol must be made or authorised by a personal licence holder.
- A premises must have a Designated Premises Supervisor (DPS) holding a valid personal licence.
- Door supervisors are to be licensed by the Security Industry Authority (SIA).
- There will be no irresponsible drink promotions that are a significant risk to the promotion of the four licensing objectives.
- Free drinking water is to be made available to guests on request.
- An age verification policy (e.g. 'challenge 21').
- Minimum drink measures are available and advertised to guests (beer or cider: ½ pint; gin, rum, vodka or whisky: 25ml or 35 ml; still wine in a glass: 125ml).
- Alcohol cannot be sold for less than the permitted price. The permitted price = the duty chargeable in relation to the alcohol added to the amount of that duty multiplied by the VAT (20%).

Venue Specific Conditions

A premises licence can also be subject to further specific conditions. These are attached to the licence in two ways:
1. Operating Schedule Conditions – submitted by the applicant.
2. Conditions Imposed at a Licensing Hearing – added by the licensing committee following a hearing for an application for a new grant, variation, or review.

Conditions should only be imposed on a licence if it is necessary to promote the licensing objectives. These can include restricting the hours for licensable activities and areas of a premises where they can take place.

Late licensed venues in some licensing authorities have many venue-specific conditions. For example, in Westminster, it is not uncommon to find 60 plus conditions on night club premises licences. However, other licensing authorities operate a much lighter touch on conditions.

It should also be noted that some licensing authorities have standard conditions that will be applied to certain premises within their area. These can be detailed in full on the premises licence or referred to in one condition.

Example Licence Conditions

Some examples of commonly found premises licence conditions are given below. This is by no means a comprehensive or exhaustive list but will give you an idea of what can be expected.

General

The premises shall install and maintain a comprehensive CCTV system as per the minimum requirements of the Police Licensing Team. All entry and exit points will be covered enabling frontal identification of every person entering in any light condition. The CCTV system shall continually record whilst the premises is open for licensable activities and during all times when customers remain on the premises. All recordings shall be stored for a minimum period of 31 days with date and time stamping. Viewing of recordings shall be made available immediately upon the request of police or authorised officers throughout the preceding 31-day period.

No noise shall emanate from the premises nor vibration be transmitted through the structure of the premises which gives rise to a nuisance.

Notices shall be prominently displayed at all exits requesting patrons to respect the needs of local residents and businesses and leave the area quietly.

Substantial food and non-intoxicating beverages, including drinking water, shall be available in all parts of the premises where alcohol is sold or supplied for consumption on the premises.

Nightclubs

A minimum of (X) SIA licensed door supervisors shall be on duty at the premises at all times whilst it is open for business.

All persons entering or re-entering the premises shall be searched by an SIA trained member of staff and monitored by the premises CCTV system.

The number of persons permitted in the premises at any one time (including staff) shall not exceed (X) persons.

Restaurants

The supply of alcohol at the premises shall only be to a person seated taking a table meal there and for consumption by such a person as ancillary to their meal.

The supply of alcohol shall be by waiter or waitress service only.

All tables and chairs shall be removed from the outside area by 23.00 hours each day.

Off Licences and Supermarkets

All sales of alcohol for consumption off the premises shall be in sealed containers only and shall not be consumed on the premises.

No super-strength beer, lagers, ciders, or spirit mixtures of 5.5% ABV (alcohol by volume) or above shall be sold at the premises, except for premium beers and ciders supplied in glass bottles.

Outside of the hours authorised for the sale of alcohol and whilst the premises are open to the public, the licence holder shall ensure that all alcohol within the premises (including alcohol behind the counter) is secured in a locked storeroom or behind locked grilles, locked screens, or locked cabinet doors so as to prevent access to the alcohol by both customers and staff.

Penalties for breaches

According to section 136 of the Licensing Act 2003, a person commits an offence if:

1. They carry on or attempt to carry on a licensable activity on or from any premises otherwise than under and in accordance with an authorisation, or
2. They knowingly allow a licensable activity to be so carried on.

The penalty is 6 months prison and/or an unlimited fine if convicted.

Potentially, anybody can commit an offence, not necessarily just the licence holder. Also, the offence does not just mean operating without a licence but also includes operating in *breach* of a licence condition, for example, staying open beyond the permitted times.

Breaches of licence conditions could also result in a review of the premises licence where further conditions or restrictions could be imposed on the licence or the licence could be suspended or revoked.

CHAPTER 2
The Importance of the Four Licensing Objectives

"Each objective is of equal importance. There are no other statutory licensing objectives, so that the promotion of the four objectives is a paramount consideration at all times."
- Revised Guidance issued under section 182 of the Licensing Act 2003 (2015)

The licensing objectives are the foundation on which The Licensing Act 2003 is built. The licensing objectives are the rationale for all the decision making of the licensing authorities and are the only grounds for regulatory intervention.

Put simply, any action taken against any premises can only be taken for an actual failure or perceived failure of the licensee to promote one or more of the licensing objectives.

This means that promoting the licensing objectives must be at the forefront of everything you do. You have a clear responsibility not just to note what they are but through actions, policies, and procedures actively promote them.

Your whole team always need to be on the same page; they are expected to know what the objectives are and how they can help you promote them.

The local licensing authority also carries out its functions to promote the licensing objectives.

What are the Four Licensing Objectives?
1. The prevention of crime and disorder
2. Public safety
3. The prevention of public nuisance
4. The protection of children from harm

How do we Promote the Licensing Objectives?

The Act does not specifically outline how to promote the objectives, but you are expected to create an operating schedule when you apply for a premises licence which, among other things, outlines how you will promote the objectives.

The four objectives cover very broad areas. In fact, pretty much any problem you might face will fall into one (or more) of the four categories. So, it's imperative that your operating policies and procedures are robust and clearly promote best practices and the four licensing objectives.

It is crucial that any incident, particularly if it was serious, is reviewed with consideration of whether the objectives were being promoted. If it could be argued that they were not, remedial action should be taken immediately and documented in detail. This should become a routine practice adopted by all managers.

Through years of being expert witnesses and having been involved in hundreds of hearings and court cases, we have a clear picture of what actions are expected and our Responsible Alcohol Service and Promoting the Four Licensing Objectives course (RASPFLO™) really brings home how crucial this area is to the staff.

Here are the highlights from the RASPFLO™ course:

All Four Objectives
- Operational policies and procedures need to be in place
- Staff training should be undertaken regularly – we suggest every six months
- Responsible alcohol sales must always be made

Prevention of Crime and Disorder
- CCTV needs to be adequate and in full working order

- Door supervisors need to be badged and in adequate numbers for the risk
- Bag clips in place to prevent theft
- Risk assessment of promoted events needs to be undertaken
- Admission policy in place that should be discerning
- Queue management in place to prevent trouble from brewing
- Polycarbonate glassware should be considered if there is a risk of assault
- Conflict management training for staff should be provided
- Drugs policy in place and enforced
- Search and seizure policy to be considered
- Cloakroom availability for large events
- Toilet checks and or attendant to be considered in what is usually a drugs hot spot
- Design out crime by improved lighting
- Staff to conduct property patrol for unattended items
- A dispersal policy in place to minimise the risk of anti-social behaviour occurring

Public Safety
- Health and safety policy
- Risk assessments
- First aiders and first aid equipment
- Means of escape – checked that they are free and unobstructed
- Glass collection
- Capacity management
- Cleaning up spillages
- Fire alarm/fire safety equipment
- Building maintenance
- Good lighting
- Temperature management

Prevention of Public Nuisance
- Noise limiter
- Extraction fan filters
- Sweeping up litter outside
- Contact number for residents
- Signage
- Door supervisors

- Queue management
- Dispersal policy
- Provision of taxis
- Travel information
- Plant and machinery well attenuated

Protection of Children from Harm
- Age checks – operate a Challenge 21 policy
- ID scan
- Signage
-

The Consequences of Failing to Promote the Licensing Objectives

Failure to adopt good practice and promote the licensing objectives can lead to a review of the licence. All licence reviews must be based on one or more objectives not being met and can happen at any time.

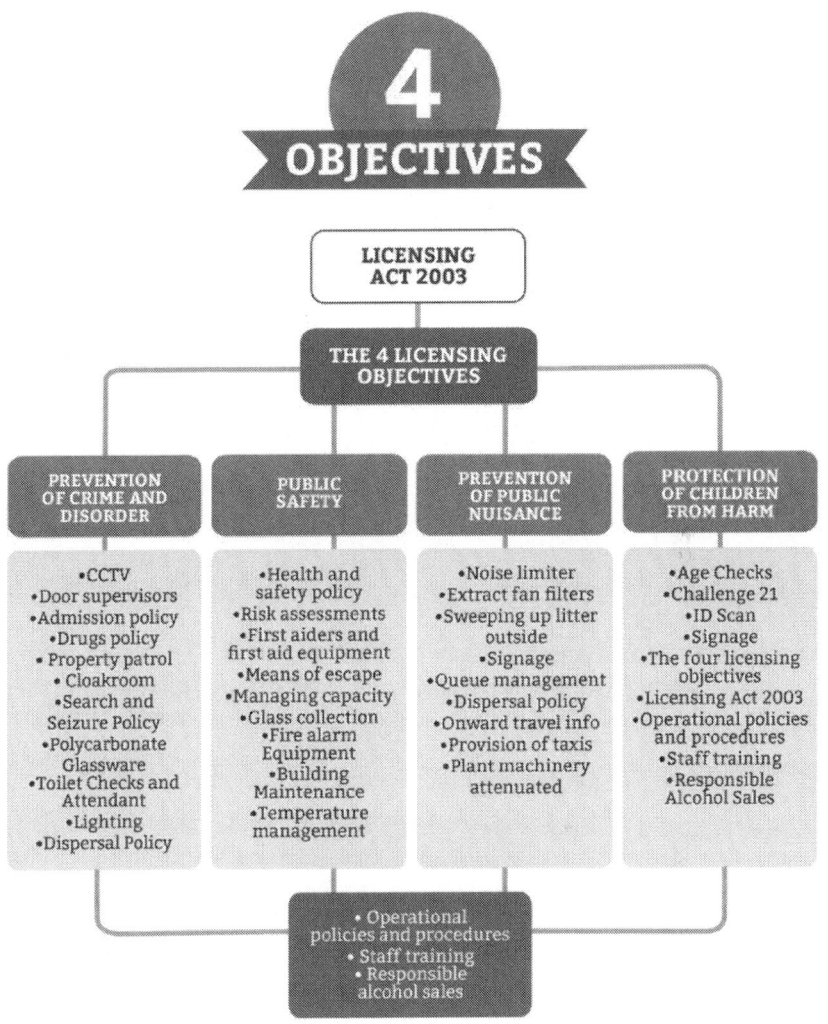

CHAPTER 3
The Problems Operators Face

"A problem is a chance for you to do your best."
- Duke Ellington

The problems operators face are numerous. On top of that, the various enforcement agencies are well-funded, experienced, and have excellent support systems and partnerships. They have extremely high expectations of activities and actions from the venue management team based on a wide variety of experience dealing with multiple premises and knowledge of the law.

Licences can be reviewed by almost anybody providing they cite one or more of the licensing objectives as grounds, which means going to a committee hearing. Councillors – who are elected by residents – chair and sit on committee hearings that decide on the fate of premises licences. They decide whether they are revoked, conditions changed, new conditions added, or even suspended.

When we deal with issues in premises, we usually find a similar pattern regardless of the size. These are the same things the authorities find when they inspect or review the premises licence.

From the side of the premises, issues are often due to an inexperienced team in place, particularly among the more junior members of the team. But this isn't the only issue we consistently find. The table below outlines examples of the gap in expectation and delivery.

WHAT AUTHORITIES EXPECT TO FIND	WHAT THEY OFTEN FIND
Policies and procedures	Lack of policies and procedures
Robust alcohol service training regime	Lack of any serious training
Incident records and statements	Incidents are not recorded / reported
Personal Licence holders to have their personal licences on them	Personal licence holders cannot produce their Personal Licence cards
A full copy of the licence	A missing Part A
Full records of refusals	No records of refusals
Guest in a salubrious state	Guest in an intoxicated state
Staff that can recite the Four Licensing Objectives	Most staff cannot recite the four licensing objectives
Plans that match the layout as per the licence	Alterations have been made and the licencing plans not updated.
Opening and closing check lists	Complete lack of paperwork
WAVE (Welfare and Vulnerability Engagement) training to have been carried out	Most premises have not undertaken any WAVE (Welfare and Vulnerability Engagement) training
CCTV working and maintained	Camera views obscured; CCTV not retained for appropriate period of time. No checks to ensure system is working correctly
Fire exits clear	Means of escape obstructed. No recorded safety checks
Safety equipment maintained	No annual tests. Equipment tampered with or in poor condition. Not positioned correctly
Risk assessments	No current risk assessments in place or risk assessments that are not being followed

10 Common Mistakes

We have created a list below of the most common mistakes made by operators. The list was compiled by canvassing licensing officers and working in partnership with the various licensing enforcement officers and teams.

1. Not knowing the difference between the premises licence and premises licence summary

Licences are issued by way of two documents: the premises licence (part A) and the licence summary (part B). The summary is the part that must be displayed prominently on the premises. The licence is a longer version of the summary and contains all the conditions; it does need to be displayed but must be produced if requested by an authorised officer.

2. Staff working at premises being unaware of licence conditions

Staff given responsibility for running licensed premises often report that they have never been made aware of the licence conditions. Ensure staff are informed of all relevant conditions and ask them to sign a confirmation that they have read and understood the conditions. If you are not always at the premises you should delegate responsibility for producing the licence to authorised officers and display a notice naming the responsible persons.

3. Not having adequate arrangements in place to operate and maintain your CCTV

Many premises will have a licence condition requiring the installation and maintenance of CCTV. If so, you should have sufficient people trained to operate the system; ideally, staff should be asked to "sign off" once they have been trained. The system should also be maintained by way of routine recorded checks confirming correct date and time, 'burn facilities' are working, and the amount of recorded material being stored is adequate (e.g. a minimum of 31 days). A log should also be kept of any faults and remedial work.

4. Inadequate due diligence record keeping

Always keep a record of your due diligence. It's evidence that you are a responsible operator and demonstrates you are proactive in managing your premises and promoting the four licensing objectives. Records should be clear and legible.

5. Failure to properly deal with incidents

You should have written policies in place and be able to evidence that staff have been trained to know when to call the police, when to preserve possible crime scenes, how to detain suspects, and how to write meaningful reports and collate evidence.

6. Failure to maintain the premises licence

If the annual fee is not paid when due, your licence can be suspended. Make a note of your fee due date and make sure it is paid in plenty of time.

You also have a legal duty to inform your local licensing authority of any change of name or address to the premises licence holder or the DPS. It is also good practice to inform them of any change to your contact details, such as email and telephone number, so you can be easily contacted.

7. Obstructed means of escape

Means of escape are often used as storage areas, putting customers and employees at risk. All dedicated exit routes must be kept clear of obstructions and appropriately maintained (doors not locked and easily openable doors, free of trip and slip hazards and obstructions, adequately lit, signposted, etc.).

8. Failure to have a written fire risk assessment

All licensed premises, regardless of the number of employees, are required to have a written risk assessment. Furthermore, all safety equipment should be adequately maintained.

9. Poor management of outside areas and dispersal

It is a mistake to believe that once guests have left your premises, they are no longer your problem. Queues, smoking areas, and dispersal must be managed correctly to ensure there is no disorder or nuisance.

10. Lack of guest welfare

You and your staff should know how to identify and deal with any person considered vulnerable and, as such, at increased risk of becoming a victim of a crime or accident. You should have a written policy detailing the measures in place to ensure the welfare of guests in your premises and how they can get home safely.

SECTION 2
Prevention

CHAPTER 4
Terms of Entry

"The greatest victory is that which requires no battle."
- Sun Tzu, The Art of War

Like many expensive products, nightclubs and bars are often aspirational. In order to succeed, they need to be seen as places for people who lead luxury lifestyles to hang out. Many of our clients have built their entire business model around having likeminded guests mixing, mingling, and socialising within their premises. To maintain this credibility and to protect their premises licence, they cannot afford to weaken their brand by allowing undesirable guests in.

Most of these businesses have an ideal guest profile and will employ a door host to vet entry accordingly. Let's be honest, they target the wealthy, successful, and the beautiful.

Managing the guest's profile is crucial to the success of any business but also plays an important part in upholding the law and licensing objectives. As such, there is an obvious expectation from the authorities to vet entry to licensed premises. Clear prohibitions include:

- Drunk people
- People on or wanting to sell drugs
- Aggressive or violent people
- Solicitation
- Age

There are also many other barriers such as submitting to a search, providing ID for scanning, paying an entry fee, or committing to a minimum spend.

Many clubs have complicated guest list policies with various promoters and sub-promoters that have different allocations for their guest lists. Some may fill up before others; some may even be priced differently. Some places have a dress code and a code of conduct. These are all barriers to entry for your average club-goer.

Door staff also have long memories for troublemakers and many of these door supervisors work across multiple doors so may refuse entry to someone who has been trouble in the past.

Staff who control access to the premises and who are responsible for upholding the guest profile are effectively gatekeepers. It is a position of great responsibility but also one that has become increasingly complex in recent times.

It is important to remember that licenced premises (usually nightclubs) are private property. There is no automatic right of entry. Unfortunately, many people don't understand this and are indignant when refused entry.

There is an increasing number of cases of trial by social media and news reports carry the assumption of guilt of the premises. Most damaging is the 'no smoke without fire' philosophy that can easily be arrived at when reading dozens of negative reviews.

The Equalities Act

This act legally protects people from discrimination, meaning they cannot be refused entry based on gender, sexual orientation, race, and other protected factors outlined below.

Increasingly though, we are finding negative reviews and complaints centred around race. In many cases, the complaint is approached with an assumption that the premises is at fault — this includes the complainant, who honestly believed they were refused entry due to racial discrimination, even when the real reason was clearly explained to them.

People do not like being told no. They become disappointed, frustrated, and angry and it takes seconds to make a racial complaint or write a poor review alleging racial discrimination.

Many people do this with a clear understanding of how damaging an allegation of racial discrimination can be to a business. We have had clients being threatened with newspaper articles and social media posts intended to go viral in a bid to ruin their reputation.

There is also some evidence that complaints have increased in venues when a more proactive approach was adopted to responding and investigating allegations of discrimination.

Discrimination can *never* be tolerated but should not be used to blackmail venues into admitting an undesirable guest either.

In our BETTER Compliance system, we've included our Door Refusals Course where we give some of the science behind the admittance process and the legal framework within which we all work. If you would like to give your staff more knowledge and confidence in this area, contact us for more information or to book training.

STAYING OPEN

EQUALITY ACT 2010

This Act legally protects people from discrimination in the workplace and in wider society.

The Act offers protection to people with a number of 'protected characteristics.'
This means that discrimination or unfair treatment on the basis of these protected characteristics is now against the law in almost all cases.

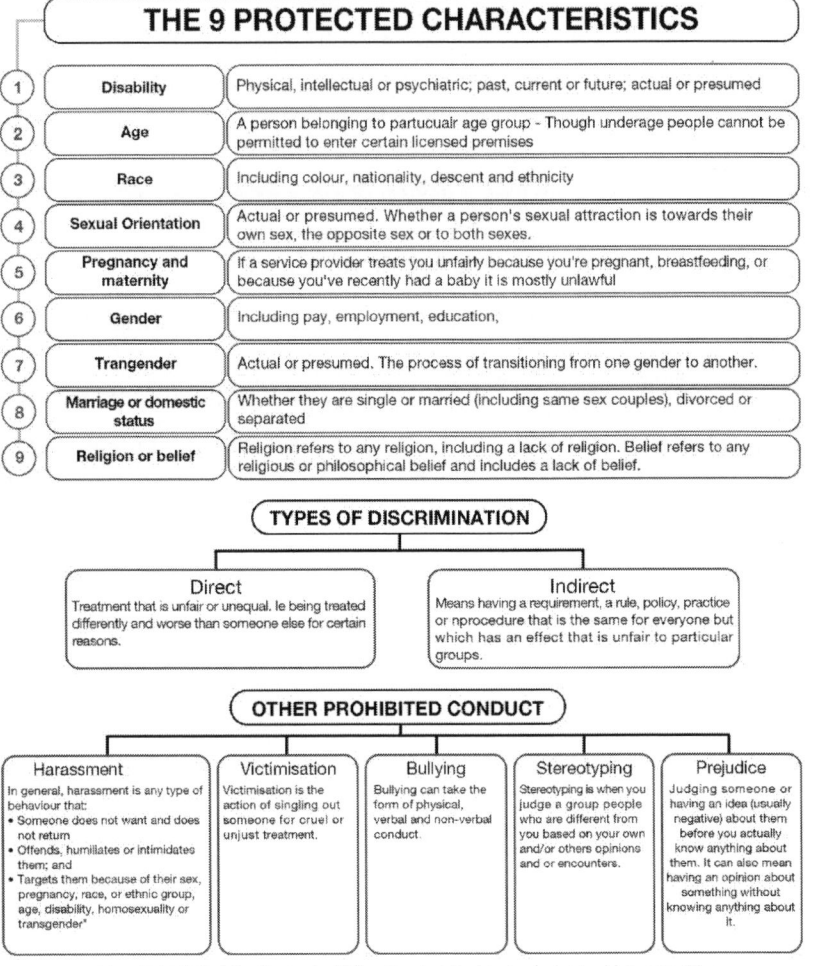

THE 9 PROTECTED CHARACTERISTICS

1	Disability	Physical, intellectual or psychiatric; past, current or future; actual or presumed
2	Age	A person belonging to particualr age group - Though underage people cannot be permitted to enter certain licensed premises
3	Race	Including colour, nationality, descent and ethnicity
4	Sexual Orientation	Actual or presumed. Whether a person's sexual attraction is towards their own sex, the opposite sex or to both sexes.
5	Pregnancy and maternity	If a service provider treats you unfairly because you're pregnant, breastfeeding, or because you've recently had a baby it is mostly unlawful
6	Gender	Including pay, employment, education,
7	Trangender	Actual or presumed. The process of transitioning from one gender to another.
8	Marriage or domestic status	Whether they are single or married (including same sex couples), divorced or separated
9	Religion or belief	Religion refers to any religion, including a lack of religion. Belief refers to any religious or philosophical belief and includes a lack of belief.

TYPES OF DISCRIMINATION

Direct
Treatment that is unfair or unequal. Ie being treated differently and worse than someone else for certain reasons.

Indirect
Means having a requirement, a rule, policy, practice or nprocedure that is the same for everyone but which has an effect that is unfair to particular groups.

OTHER PROHIBITED CONDUCT

Harassment
In general, harassment is any type of behaviour that:
- Someone does not want and does not return
- Offends, humiliates or intimidates them; and
- Targets them because of their sex, pregnancy, race, or ethnic group, age, disability, homosexuality or transgender'

Victimisation
Victimisation is the action of singling out someone for cruel or unjust treatment.

Bullying
Bullying can take the form of physical, verbal and non-verbal conduct.

Stereotyping
Stereotyping is when you judge a group people who are different from you based on your own and/or others opinions and or encounters.

Prejudice
Judging someone or having an idea (usually negative) about them before you actually know anything about them. It can also mean having an opinion about something without knowing anything about it.

Important fact: It is always lawful to treat a disabled person more favourably than a non-disabled person.

The Two-step Process of Assessing Guests

Step 1: SAAB - Speech, Appearance, Attitude, Behaviour
Does the guest appear intoxicated? It is an offence to admit anyone who

STAYING OPEN

is intoxicated onto the premises, so they need to be refused. Additionally, if someone is intoxicated you need to insist that at least one of the group stays with that person to look after them as they are now considered a potentially vulnerable person.

Are they a possible threat to the prevention of crime and disorder objective? This is largely body language driven. We worked with an NLP expert to develop some behaviours and speech patterns to look out for which we've outlined below.

Step 2: DR - Door Requirements
Do the guests meet your door entry requirements such as being on a guest list, having a table booking, etc.? Do they meet the dress code?

In the flow chart below there is a list of entry requirements that you should have in place that all guest should be able to meet to gain admission.

STAYING OPEN

Factors Associated with Admittance
PRIMARY ASSESSMENT
Is the person too intoxicated to allow entry? Assessed Under SAAB

Remember- If someone is too intoxicated to allow entry you must refuse entry to another person in party to ensure the intoxicated person is looked after and wont come to possible harm

POSITIVES

SPEECH		APPEARANCE	
Normal Speech (be aware some people have speech impediment - this is not a negative)		Eyes are Normal	
Appropriate Volume		Face Looks normal	
Consitent Volume		Eyes are open	
Cohenrent Thought process		Focussed when spoken to	
Normal Response time		Not overly sweaty	
Rational Speech		Clothing looks good	

ATTITUDE		BEHAVIOUR	
Friendly		Open, friendly behaviour	
Conciliatory		Standing and walking straight	
Respecting Boundaries		In Good Mood	
Open/Friendly		Consisteant behaviour	
Happy Demenour		Relaxed Shoulders	
		Alert	
		In Control	
		Can Answer questions	
		Calm and Still	
		Seek Diffuse	

NEGATIVES

SPEECH		APPEARANCE		ATTITUDE	
Thick, slurred speech		Bloodshot, glassy eyes		Argumentative	
Loud, noisy speech		Flushed face		Aggressive or belligerent	
Speaking loudly, then quietly		Droopy eyelids		Obnoxious or mean	
Rambling train of thought		Dazed look		Inappropriate sexual advances	
Slow response to questions or comments		Body tremors		Overly friendly to other guests or employees	
Bravado, boasting		Blank stare		Boisterous	
Making irrational statements		Sweaty Forehead		Overconfidence	
Repeating themselves		Excessive Sweating		Depressed or sullen	
Incoherent		Disheveled clothing		Moody	
Crude, inappropriate speech or gestures		Odour of alcohol, marijuana or chemicals			

BEHAVIOUR			
Swaying, staggering, or stumbling		Drowsiness/Falling asleep	
Unable to stand straight		Lack of focus and eye contact	
Clumsy/Careless with money		Difficulty standing up/Falling Over	
Restless		Falling down	
Emotional/Crying /Laughing Hysterically		Difficulty lighting cigarettes	
Extreme or sudden change in behavior		Difficulty remembering, Disoriented	
Overly animated or entertaining		Agitated, anxious/Grinding Teeth	

STAYING OPEN

Factors Associated with Admittance
SECONDARY ASSESSMENT
Based on two points
DRSAAB

1. Do they also meet the Door entry requirements of the premises?
2. Could this person be a threat to the Prevention of Crime and Disorder objective - Assessed under SAAB?

POSITIVES

DOOR ENTRY REQUIREMENTS
- Need to Have ID
- Happy to be searched
- Mixed Group
- On the guest List
- Promoters Guest List Not Full
- Fits the Dress Code
- Can Afford a Table
- Group Arrival
- ID Scan Positive
- Security Happy
- Meets Age Requirement
- Do Not Discriminate Ever

SPEECH
- Conversational
- Conversational responses
- Normal tone
- Open speech style
- Friendly answers
- Direct answers
- Appropriate Volume
- Fluid Speech when answering
- No Excessive bad language

APPEARANCE
- Relaxed appearance
- Consistent movement
- Maintaining a relaxed appearance
- Making eye contact
- Maintaining eye contact
- Open, symmetrical posture
- Relaxed Demenour
- Suitably Attired

ATTITUDE
- Friendly
- Conciliatory
- Passive
- Open/Friendly
- Calm Demenour

BEHAVIOUR
- Open, friendly behaviour
- Happy/Neutral
- Maintaining demeanour
- Normal Breathing
- Relaxed Shoulders

- Relaxed Body Shape
- Eyes Normal
- Seek Rapport
- Relaxed Calm and Still
- Seek Diffuse

NEGATIVES

DOOR ENTRY REQUIREMENTS
- No Id or Reluctant
- Refuses to be searched
- Single Sex Group
- Not on Guest List
- Promoters Guest List Full
- Unsuitable Clothing
- Cant Afford a Table
- Single Arrival
- ID Scan Red Flag
- Known Trouble Maker
- Previous Problem at Venue
- Security Express Concern
- Not Old Enough

SPEECH
- Clipped tone
- Mono-syllabic responses
- Quiet tone
- Closed speech pattern
- Defensive answers -
- Answering a question with a question
- Inappropriate Volume Eg Shouting
- Hesitating when answering
- Crude, inappropriate speech or gestures

ATTITUDE
- Aggressive
- Argumentative
- Easily angered or quick to anger
- Evasive
- Overly Boisterous
- Overconfidence
- Depressed or sullen
- Moody

APPEARANCE
- Stiff posture
- Sudden movements
- Sudden alertness
- Not making eye contact
- Glancing
- Asymmetric posture
- Nervous/figity
- Not Suitable Attired

BEHAVIOUR
- Evasive behaviour
- Angry
- Changing behaviour when confronted
- Deep breath in
- Pulling shoulder back
- Making themselves appear bigger/Tension
- Narrowing/Widening of Eyes
- Seek Confrontation
- Moving (backwards or forwards)
- Seek to escalate

37

Factors Associated with Admittance

THING TO SAY AND NOT SAY TO GUEST

POSITIVES — Do Say
- Be polite and empathise – "I am so sorry and this must be a real disappointment but..."
- Flatter and charm – "guys you look great tonight but unfortunately..."
- Be credible and use a realistic and believable reason for refusal – "I'm sorry but the paying guest list is full now and we are only allowing admittance to guests with table reservations"
- Soften the blow – "...but please come back next week...."
- Opt for refusal by upselling – "I am afraid the guest list is full but you can have a table for £3000"
- Explain clearly – "Our guest list doesn't allow trainers – it will have been sent with your reservation confirmation and is also published on our website"
- Remember - be aware other guests are listening

NEGATIVES — Don't Say
- Anything considered personal remarks i.e. insulting – "guys you don't have the right look for us"
- Single out one person – "you three are ok but she's not right"
- Humiliate – "you've got to be joking – not in a millions years, mate"
- Obvious lies – "we're full" (and then let 10 people in) or "come back next week" (if there is no way they will get in then either)
- Complicated explanations – "you see you're on Tom's list who has 20 paying at £20 and 10 at £20 and 10 comps, but he's already had 25 guests in so that list is almost closed but he's not here and I don't know if he has other people coming not on this list...."
- Remember – don't immediately contradict what you have just said to one guest when dealing with the next guest in the queue

Social and Moral Issues

Whilst some forms of discrimination are not unlawful, there is a moral responsibility to avoid discriminating against characteristics such as body size and attractiveness. Doing so is offensive and socially unacceptable. It is important that anyone vetting entry is respectful and handles refusals sensitively.

Example Policy

"The aim of this policy is to prevent problems inside the premises by ensuring that the highest standards are in place when vetting guests prior to them entering.

STAYING OPEN

It is especially important that there is a consistent standard and approach to whom is allowed on the premises.

The following controls on entry will be implemented by managers, door hosts, and security at the entrance.

The following persons will be refused entry:
1. *Any persons deemed by management or security to be under the influence of alcohol or illegal substances*
2. *Any persons carrying or thought to be carrying any form of offensive weapon*
3. *Any person who refuses to be searched when asked*
4. *Any person who refuses to provide ID when asked*
5. *Any persons not in keeping with the dress code, set out below*
6. *Any persons who are known to have been involved in any criminal activities either within or in the areas surrounding the premises*
7. *Any ex-employees of the business whose employment was terminated by the company*

The Premises reserves the right to search customers and scan IDs as a condition of entry to ensure the safety of both customers and staff.

<u>Guest Dress Code</u>
- *Smart casual dress*
- *If customers are wearing caps, these are to be removed on entry.*

Management reserve the right of entry. Being on a guest list or having a table reservation does not guarantee entry."

CHAPTER 5
Young People

"When you turn 18, you can legally do all the things you've been doing since you were 15."

- Anon

The above quote is intended to be humorous, but it voices a stark reality; many young people who have not reached the legal age to purchase alcohol frequently attempt to drink in licensed premises.

The law states that you can *never* knowingly sell alcohol to people under the age of 18. It's an offence and if you're found guilty you are liable for an unlimited fine.

There is only one occasion on which you can *serve* alcohol to children under the age of 18 – when a 16 or 17-year-old is consuming a meal in a restaurant with a responsible adult. The 16 or 17-year-old can only have beer, cider, or wine and the adult must pay for the alcohol.

Under the Licensing Act 2003, all licensed premises are subject to the mandatory condition of a strictly enforced age verification policy. It's best practice to operate a 'Challenge 21' or 'Challenge 25' policy where any guest appearing under 21 or 25 is required to provide proof of age. This should be followed by everyone serving alcohol and, in some venues, enforced at the entrance by security.

All staff are responsible for checking the age of your customers. Never assume that a co-worker has checked effectively as you will put yourself at risk of serving someone underage.

Have clear and prominent signage of your age policy at the entrance, on your website, and any promotional material to advise guests that ID will be required. For example: "If you look under 21 you will be asked to prove you are 18."

Acceptable ID includes a valid driver's licence with a photo, a valid passport, proof of age standards scheme or (PASS) approved cards, and military ID.

Methods of Checking ID
We suggest using the T-L-A method to ensure that a person's ID is valid:
- Touch for alterations — bumps, cracks, or slits
- Look at the date of birth and the photo to ensure it is the correct person
- Ask questions to confirm that the ID is theirs. You could ask for their postcode, star sign, or for secondary ID like a bank card.

Remember: if you have any doubts about the ID, DON'T ACCEPT IT!

The Home Office advises that any fake IDs should be retained and destroyed. As well as fake IDs, many underage people use real IDs of siblings or friends. If it is a real ID belonging to a friend or sibling, it should be confiscated and the person producing it told that the real owner can collect it.

Any person using a fake or another person's identity documents commits a criminal offence under the Identity Documents Act 2010. If they are using a false document to obtain alcohol, they commit an offence under the Licensing Act 2003 and the Fraud Act 2006. Furthermore, any person forging or altering a passport commits an offence under the Forgery and Counterfeiting Act 1981.

Offences Under the Licensing Act 2003
There are numerous offences involving the sale of alcohol to children:

Section 145(1)
It is an offence to allow unaccompanied under-16-year-olds on relevant premises at a time when alcohol is being supplied. The offence is committed by any person authorised to request under 16s to leave premises and a person guilty of an offence under this section is liable on summary conviction to a maximum fine of £1000.

Section 146
It is an offence to sell alcohol to a child under 18. A club commits an offence under section 146(2) if alcohol is supplied by it or on its behalf to, or to the order of, a member of the club who is under 18.

A person charged with an offence because of their own conduct has the same defence available as for section 145 charge – the person charged had no reason to suspect that the individual was under 16. A person charged because of their act, or default of another, also has a due diligence defence available.

Offences committed under Section 145 and 146 share a defence that they had no reason to suspect the person was under 16. This is where due diligence becomes very important; you should be able to demonstrate that you have procedures in place to prevent underage people from gaining access.

Section 147
It is an offence to knowingly allow the sale of alcohol, on relevant premises, to a child under 18. Here, the offence would not be committed if the child unwittingly consumed a spiked drink.

A person guilty of an offence under section 146 or 147 is liable on summary conviction to an unlimited fine.

Mandatory Conditions
Every premises licence that authorises the sales of alcohol is subject to a mandatory condition requiring an age verification policy.

1. *The premises licence holder or club premises certificate holder must ensure that an age verification policy is adopted in respect of the premises in relation to the sale or supply of alcohol.*
2. *The designated premises supervisor in relation to the premises licence must ensure that the supply of alcohol at the premises is carried on in accordance with the age verification policy.*
3. *The policy must require individuals who appear to the responsible person to be under 18 years of age (or such older age as may be specified in the policy) to produce on request, before being served alcohol, identification bearing their photograph, date of birth and either (a) a holographic mark, or (b) an ultraviolet feature.*

Venue Specific Conditions

In addition to the mandatory age verification condition, your premises may also be subject to venue specific conditions that outline time restraints for when persons under the age of 18 are allowed in the premises or that all tills need to automatically prompt staff to ask for age verification identification when presented with an alcohol sale. Any conditions should be incorporated into your age verification policy and staff training.

Example of an Age Policy

"The following procedures will be implemented by managers, door hosts and security at the entrance, and by serving staff at the point of sale.

1. *The premises operates a strict 'Challenge 25' policy where any guest appearing under 25 will be required to provide proof of age.*
2. *The premises does not allow unaccompanied under-18-year-olds on the premises. Any person under 18 must be accompanied by a responsible adult.*
3. *The premises does not allow under-16-year-olds on the premises after 20:00 hours*
4. *This policy is enforced at the entrance by security and managers.*
5. *Only international passports, UK driving licences, or any PASS approved proof of age card will be accepted as proof of age.*
6. *When checking ID staff will: -*
   - *Check the 3D effect hologram is not stuck on*
   - *Check photo to ensure it is the correct person*
   - *Check date of birth*
   - *Check ID for any tampering*
   - *If unsure of the person's age, refuse service/entry*

IF A GUEST CANNOT PROVIDE SATISFACTORY PROOF OF AGE, ENTRY WILL BE DENIED AND THEY WILL BE REMINDED TO BRING PROOF OF AGE IN FUTURE

1. *There will be clear and prominent signage displayed at the entrance advising guests of the age policy and that 'if you look under 25 you will be asked to prove you are 18'.*
2. *The age policy will be displayed on the premises' website and any promotional material.*

3. *The premises will keep a written record each night of guests who are refused entry or service at the bar.*
4. *Staff serving alcohol must also question a customer's age if they feel that they may not be 18 years of age using the 'challenge 25' policy."*

Remember that underage people are considered vulnerable. Your guest welfare policy should also cover how to protect and provide for their care.

STAYING OPEN

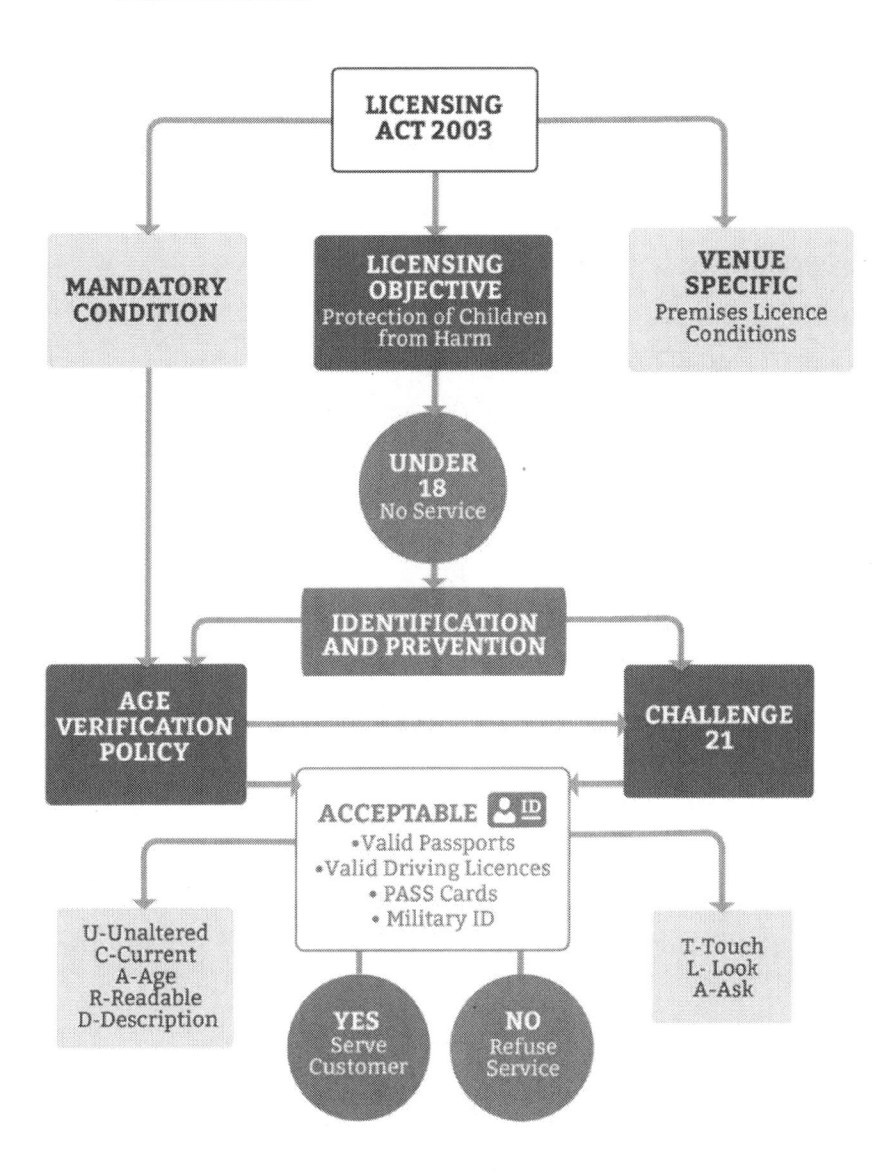

AGE VERIFICATION

LICENSING ACT 2003

- **MANDATORY CONDITION**
- **LICENSING OBJECTIVE** — Protection of Children from Harm
- **VENUE SPECIFIC** — Premises Licence Conditions

UNDER 18 — No Service

IDENTIFICATION AND PREVENTION

- **AGE VERIFICATION POLICY**
- **CHALLENGE 21**

ACCEPTABLE
- Valid Passports
- Valid Driving Licences
- PASS Cards
- Military ID

U - Unaltered
C - Current
A - Age
R - Readable
D - Description

T - Touch
L - Look
A - Ask

YES — Serve Customer

NO — Refuse Service

CHAPTER 6
Search/Seizure

"In the midst of the disguises and artifices that reign among men, it is only attention and vigilance that can save us from surprises."
- Jacques-Benigne Bossuet

A rather grand quote with an important message and keyword – vigilance. Unfortunately, some people may wish to bring illegal items into your premises for a variety of reasons. It might be drugs for personal use, or to deal to other guests; it might be a weapon for self-defence or carried with intent to harm a specific person or persons; it could simply be a case of someone bringing in their own alcohol to avoid purchasing yours.

Whatever the reason, your search policy must prevent any of these items from coming into your venue.

All late licensed premises (and some others that employ security) are expected to have a search policy as part of the entry and vetting process. The aim of any search policy is to prevent prohibited items being brought into a premises. In this context, prohibited items would fall into the following categories:
- Weapons (including bombs and acid)
- Non-prescription drugs
- Alcohol

Your search procedures must be:
- Effective
- Consistent
- Fair

- Transparent

The Searching Basics

Your first task is to identify the risks – what is the most likely prohibitive article people will attempt to bring into your premises? For instance, whilst you will need to cover all the bases, your search regime may be different if the priority is drugs rather than weapons and vice versa.

You should inform your guests that being searched is a condition of entry to your premises with signage prominently placed at the entrance and/or queuing area. Information should also be included with ticket and marketing information.

Some venues decide to search everyone entering their premises, others adopt a random policy. Whatever policy you decide to implement, it should be based on your risk assessment of the activity taking place. It is also worth noting that many late licensed premises are subject to licence conditions requiring searching.

Example Notice

"This premises operates a search policy. All persons entering the premises may be subject to a search of outer clothing and personal belongings. This is a condition of entry. Those unwilling to be searched will be refused admittance. Any illegal drugs or weapons will be seized and the police notified. By order of the management."

People must consent to being searched but if they refuse, you are entirely within your rights to refuse admission.

All searches of customers should take place in a well-lit area clearly covered by CCTV. Security should ask guests to empty their own pockets and it's good practice to provide a table or other flat surface for them to place their property on.

Searches should take place before any entrance fee payment. This way, if they are deemed unsuitable for entry you don't have to deal with issuing a refund.

All physical searches must be same-sex (i.e. male security to search male guests and female security to search female guests). Security must be sensitive to a person's gender or the gender with which they identify. If in doubt, security should ask who the guest would prefer to search them.

Physical searches can only be of outer clothing. Bags may be opened and searched but security should avoid handling guests' property. Ask the person being searched to remove their own property – this reduces the risk of sharps injuries and allegations of property theft.

Searching for Weapons

The vast majority of weapons are metal (although those searching should be mindful that others are not, for example, ceramic knives and acid). Accordingly, if there is a high risk of persons bringing weapons to your premises, searching should include metal detecting devices such as wands and/or arches. These types of equipment must be properly calibrated and tested regularly to ensure they are operating correctly.

Searches with metal detecting devices should still be supported by physical searches. If the wand or arch shows an alert (or at the discretion of staff), then a physical pat-down search should be carried out and guests asked to empty their pockets.

Searching for Drugs

If the aim of your search policy is to prevent drugs being brought into your venue, a thorough physical search will be necessary. But those searching must do so within the legal limits by only searching outer clothing and bags.

Seizure

So, what do you do if a search discovers a prohibited item? The item should be seized following the correct protocols. Most importantly, **you should call the police (or follow the agreed protocol with your local police) in any case where a weapon or drug dealing is involved or suspected.**

In the event of seizure of a weapon or drugs:

- Ensure the process is witnessed.
- Confiscate the item found.
- Record and log details of the item found in the drugs or weapons register (see below).
- Place drugs in an evidence bag (often provided by police) or sealed envelope, signed across the seal.

- Place knives or sharp objects in a safe container or weapons tube (often provided by police).
- In the event of a large quantity of drugs or a weapon being found, call the police immediately.
- Where possible, the suspect should be detained (subject to the safety of staff and guests).

All seizures should be recorded and it is recommended that you have a detailed drugs and weapons register to evidence that any confiscated items were held and disposed of properly. The registers should contain the following information:
- Date and time
- Where found
- Details of the person who found the item and any witnesses
- Description of item
- A unique reference number
- Any action taken (e.g. person detained, police called)
- Signature of person seizing
- Signature of manager
- Details of the person searched (if available)

Premises Licence Conditions

Finally, some premises licences may be subject to conditions relating to searching (for example, that it is a condition of entry). Any conditions should be incorporated into your search policy and staff training.

CHAPTER 7
Preventing and Dealing with Intoxication

"By drinking, a boy acts like a man. After drinking, many a man acts like a boy."

- Mokokoma Mokhonoana

Controlling the consumption of alcohol in guests is one of the main issues most venues face. The very thing that you sell is the same thing that gets you into trouble when you sell too much.

To put it into perspective, here are some stats:
- Every year, over a million people in the UK are admitted to A&E with an alcohol-related injury or illness.
- It is estimated the annual cost of alcohol to the UK economy is in the £20billion region.
- In the year ending March 2018, 39% of all victims of violence in England and Wales said their attacker was affected by alcohol at the time.
- It is estimated that there were 561,000 violent alcohol-related incidents in 2017.
- Alcohol misuse is a factor in 30% of suicides each year.

Both you and your staff should understand the effects of alcohol on the body, how you can identify and deal with intoxicated guests, and methods to prevent intoxication.

It's safe to say that most serious incidents in licensed premises are, in one way or another, due to intoxication. Intoxicated guests are far more likely to cause trouble and are also far more likely to become victims of crime or accidents.

As such, it is an offence under the Licensing Act 2003 to knowingly sell alcohol to a drunk person and allow disorderly conduct on licensed premises – you could incur a hefty fine for doing so.

It's a strange paradox – you are in the business of selling alcohol but are unable, by law, to sell too much to anyone. This is contrary to the normal way of business where it's natural to sell as much of your product as you can. However, having intoxicated guests is not good for business as they cause problems and spoil the enjoyment of other guests.

Effects of Alcohol and Identifying Intoxication

Alcohol is a powerful chemical that can have a wide range of adverse effects on almost every part of your body, including your brain, bones, and heart.

It is very important that you and your staff understand the effects of alcohol and can identify a person who is becoming intoxicated. To do this, you can use our easy 4-step **SAAB** process:
- Speech
- Appearance
- Attitude
- Behaviour

Within these four key areas, there are many signs to look out for that can help you detect if someone is becoming intoxicated.

If a person shows one or two of these signs, that does not necessarily mean the person is intoxicated. However, a combination of many of these and a sudden change in behaviour is a strong indication.

All staff should understand that if you are not sure – don't serve!

The below table summarises the effects of alcohol on the body, depending on how many units have been consumed. Remember, this is based on someone with a normal tolerance to alcohol.

Alcohol Units	Effect
1-2 Units	- Increased heart rate - Blood vessels expand with a feeling of warmth - Increased sociability and talking
4-6 Units	- Brain and nervous system affected - Judgement and decision making impaired, causing recklessness and inhibition - Feeling lightheaded - Reduced reaction times and co-ordination
8-9 Units	- Reaction times much slower - Slurred speech - Blurred vision - Hangover likely (too much alcohol for your liver to remove overnight)
10-12 Units	- Co-ordination highly impaired - Drowsiness - Alcohol reaching toxic levels – increased urination, dehydration, and headaches - Upset digestion – nausea, vomiting, diarrhoea, and indigestion
13+ Units	- Considerable risk of alcohol poisoning leading to breathing, heart rate, and gag reflex difficulties - Risk of coma and death

Intervention Strategies

Intervention is the plan of action you and your staff take to prevent a guest from drinking to the point of intoxication.

There are many strategies and techniques to help you intervene effectively and safely. Many managers we work with have developed their own way of doing things over the years so you must always do what you feel works best for you.

Your staff have the right to refuse alcohol service and management must create a supportive environment that encourages responsible employee practices.

Take the time to develop your refusal policy for your premises. It will make your job easier if you know what is expected of your team and give everyone more confidence in dealing with situations.

Cutting Someone Off

Cutting someone off from being served more alcohol can be difficult, but it's important to deliver a consistent message that all guests understand. We have reviewed thousands of incidents over the years and the decision to make an intervention and cut someone off or remove them from the premises is a major flashpoint in many of them.

Whatever the situation, it needs to be handled delicately. Read the situation in front of you; the type of guest, size of group, and the vibe they have been giving off. Tell another manager or security of what you intend to do so that they can stand at a distance relative to the danger of the situation and put your conflict management training at the front of your mind.

A professional attitude and approach when refusing service keeps you in control of the situation. Here are some simple guidelines you can follow to help navigate this delicate situation.

- Identify the informal leader of the group or the person in charge. Take the time to speak to them about what you are going to do with one of their guests and why.
- By enlisting their support, it will not only help the situation from not escalating further but should help in de-escalating things.
- Be courteous and concerned – people are cooperative when being treated respectfully.
- Be tactful – try not to accuse a guest of being intoxicated.
- Do not embarrass or patronise the guest in front of anybody – simply say you cannot serve them alcohol at this time.
- Be firm – remain calm and do not back down or allow the guest to talk you out of your decision. If necessary, ask for assistance

STAYING OPEN

from a manager or another employee.
- Be confident – this convinces people you know what you are doing.
- Offer for the guests to get some fresh air for 10 minutes outside. Then you can decide what to do from there.

Some additional intervention tips and things to remember:
- Slow the service down to guests who are drinking rapidly
- Wait until a customer finishes a drink before offering another
- If it's bottle service, only allow staff to pour the drinks
- Before delivering a bottle, wait until most of the guests have arrived
- Keep the bottle in an ice bucket off the table
- Watch for signs of visible intoxication using SAAB (speech, attitude, appearance, behaviour)
- Encourage customers to order food
- Offer water, coffee, or other non-alcoholic spacers between drinks
- Smile, make eye contact, and have an open body language but keep a safe distance
- Chat with guest to determine their status if you need to
- Check with staff members on who has been serving the group to get the lay of the land, so to speak
- When you refuse service, tell your fellow manager and staff so everyone knows what is going on
- Take a manager or security with you when you must refuse service
- Use peer pressure when appropriate by asking for support from the customer's friends
- Offer something to eat
- Always remember your WAVE (Welfare and Vulnerability Engagement) training as you have a vulnerable person in front you
- Enter incidents relating to refusal of service in a logbook, especially those involving threats or aggression.

INTOXICATION

IDENTIFICATION

SAAB

SPEECH
- Slurred
- Loud
- Swearing
- Rambling
- Repetitive

APPEARANCE
- Bloodshot eyes
- Dishevelled clothing
- Flushed Face
- Blank Stare
- Droopy Eyelids

ATTITUDE
- Argumentative
- Aggressive
- Boisterous
- Obnoxious
- Overly Amorous
- Over Friendly

BEHAVIOUR
- Swaying
- Staggering
- Clumsy
- Vomitting
- Drowsy
- Disorientated

INTERVENTION
Refuse service

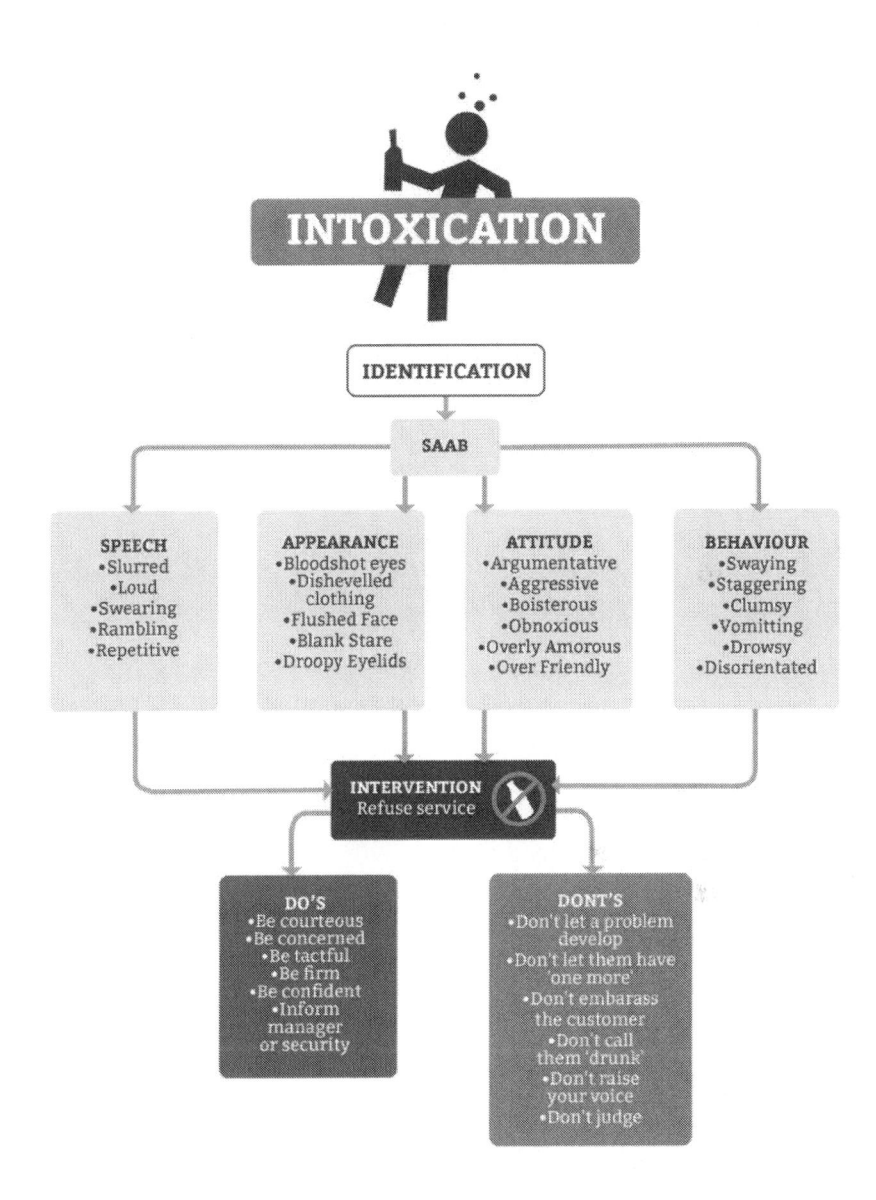

DO'S
- Be courteous
- Be concerned
- Be tactful
- Be firm
- Be confident
- Inform manager or security

DONT'S
- Don't let a problem develop
- Don't let them have 'one more'
- Don't embarass the customer
- Don't call them 'drunk'
- Don't raise your voice
- Don't judge

Factors that Affect Drinking Behaviour

Understanding the following factors will put you in a better position to promote a safe and responsible drinking culture.

The Drink

- The amount and strength of alcohol
- How it served (e.g. bottle service, shots, etc.)
- Control of pouring drinks at a table

The Drinker
- The characteristics of the person drinking the alcohol
- Their state of mind and personal circumstances
- Age, sex, weight, age, and if they have eaten all play a part in how quickly they become intoxicated

The Environment
- The atmosphere – the general mood or feeling of an establishment
- Prevailing rules of the establishment
- The layout of the premises
- Lighting and the music
- Vertical drinking (i.e., standing) has been shown to promote more rapid drinking than when people are seated

Removing or changing any one of these factors will alter the drinking behaviour. For example, a person's behaviour at a fine restaurant is likely to be very different from that person's behaviour while watching a sports game at a bar. The environment has changed, even though the exact same amount was consumed in both circumstances. Part of creating the right atmosphere is about encouraging people to behave in a manner that is in keeping with the style of your premises.

The manager and staff are in a position to control or influence at least two of the three factors above: the amount and type of drink served and, in particular, the environment.

No one factor by itself causes or can eliminate violence but having a range of protective factors and making sure there are as few risk factors as possible mean the likelihood of problems is significantly reduced.

Protective Factors When Managing the Atmosphere
- Lack of congestion, not overcrowding, and managing pinch points and hotspots such as cloakroom queues
- Inappropriate persons (e.g., intoxicated, or underage) being refused entry or refused service
- Good standards of cleanliness and housekeeping

STAYING OPEN

- Friendly staff
- Quick and efficient service
- Calling last orders in plenty of time
- Managing the exit and dispersal of patrons
- Monitoring patrons at entry, the bar, and the exit
- Promotion of food (full meals and snacks)
- Higher percentage of customers sitting
- Staff trained in responsible service
- Good range of reasonably priced soft drinks
- Good communication between staff

All these factors encourage relaxed, social drinking. Part of creating the right atmosphere is about encouraging people to behave in a manner that meets your standards and suits your premises.

DRINKING BEHAVIOUR

THE DRINK
The amount and strength of alcohol

THE DRINKER
The characteristics of the person drinking

THE ENVIRONMENT
The atmosphere and rules of the establishment

RISK FACTORS
- Not knowing the alcohol volume / unit in each drink
- Shots / Chasers Mixing drinks e.g. wine and spirits
- Free or cheap drinks
- Drinking competitions

RISK FACTORS
- Young people
- Slight build
- Females
- Empty stomach
- Not used to drinking
- Emotional
- Groups - hen / stag parties

RISK FACTORS
- Congestion / overcrowding
- Offensive Music
- Vertical drinking
- Underage allowed in
- Aggressive staff
- Passive staff
- Poor maintenance
- Lewd behaviour

LICENSING ACT 2003
The Four Licensing Objectives

PROTECTIVE FACTORS
- Minimum prescribed measures
- Responsible
- Service Policy
- Staff training

PROTECTIVE FACTORS
- Age verification policy
- Promoting food menu
- Refuse entry to inappropriate people
- Monitoring guests

PROTECTIVE FACTORS
- Well controlled
- Stop pinch points
- Seating
- Good service
- Lighting
- Good maintenance / cleanliness
- Appropriate music

CHAPTER 8
Drugs Awareness

"Drugs are a waste of time. They destroy your memory and your self-respect and everything that goes along with your self-esteem."
– Kurt Cobain

This chapter aims to introduce you to the issues relating to drug use on licensed premises, your responsibilities, and ways to identify, prevent, and understand drug use.

Unfortunately, a night out clubbing is often synonymous with drug taking in a small but significant minority of people. But allowing drug misuse demonstrates a failure to promote the licensing objectives. It is an area of zero tolerance for the authorities who see drugs within the wider picture of knife crime, gang-related violence, and people trafficking.

You need to keep your venue drug-free and communicate an anti-drug message in a clear and positive way. By allowing or turning a blind eye to drug taking or dealing, the authorities will think you are complicit in these activities and may take action against you personally as well as the premises licence.

The Need for Zero Tolerance

Every premises should have a drugs policy with the following three main aims:

1. Prevention of drug use on the premises
2. Prevention of drug dealing on the premises
3. Safeguarding those that have taken drugs

In the event of suspected drug activity, the police have two powers:

1. A review of the premises licence
2. Closure of the premises for up to 24 hours

Increasingly, police are using database and intelligence gathering techniques to target premises that are suspected of allowing this activity:

- People who are arrested can be tested for drugs.
- All people arrested are searched – not just for weapons and contraband but receipts as well. These are looked at and recorded in a database. Police build up a picture of events leading up to arrest, including what premises they were at prior to the arrest.
- Police use swabs taken on the premises during licensing inspections that are sent off analysis.
- Targeted, intelligence-led operations take place based on informants and intel gathered.
- Arrested drug dealers' phones, social media, and bank accounts are investigated.
- Ambulance calls are monitored.

The Misuse of Drugs Act 1971

This is the main piece of legislation covering drugs and their categorisation. Drugs are split into three classes (in accordance with their toxic effect), which determines the penalties for offences under the Act.

The following table sets out a summary of the potential penalties for possession and dealing controlled drugs. This may change over time as drugs get reclassified from time to time.

	Class of Drug	Possession	Dealing
A	Ecstasy, LSD, heroin, cocaine, crack, magic mushrooms, amphetamines (if prepared for injection), Opium	Up to seven years in prison or an unlimited fine or both.	Up to life in prison or an unlimited fine or both.
B	Amphetamines, Cannabis, Methylphenidate (Ritalin), Pholcodine	Up to five years in prison or an unlimited fine or both.	Up to 14 years in prison or an unlimited fine or both.
C	Tranquilisers, some painkillers, Gamma Hydroxybutyrate (GHB), Ketamine, Rohypnol (date rape drug)	Up to two years in prison or an unlimited fine or both.	Up to life in prison or an unlimited fine or both.

Offences under the Misuse of Drugs Act 1971

- Unlawful possession of a controlled drug
- Unlawful possession with intent to supply
- Supplying or offering to supply a controlled drug
- Producing or being concerned in the production
- Cultivating cannabis
- Being the occupier or concerned in the management of premises who knowingly permits or suffers certain activities to take place on those premises

> **If you knowingly allow drug offences to take place in a licensed premises, you are breaking the law.**

Psychoactive Substances Act 2016

The Psychoactive Substances Act came into force on 26 May 2016. This act makes it illegal to produce, supply, import or export any psychoactive substance (such as nitrous oxide 'laughing gas') that is likely to be used to get high.

Legal high

The term 'legal high' is commonly used to describe new psychoactive substances (NPS) but it is misleading. Many 'legal highs' (e.g. types of synthetic cannabinoids) are already controlled under the Misuse of Drugs Act, which now specifies particular drugs and groups of drugs (e.g. synthetic cannabinoids that impact on specific receptors in the brain). Many products sold as 'legal highs' contain multiple NPS and many contain illegal or banned substances.

Preventing drug use within a venue will use a combination of the following:

Staff	Environment
Training	Customer signage
Use of SIA registered door supervisors	Visible monitoring of areas
	Use of CCTV
Body and bag searches	Policies including search and seizure
Toilet attendants	
	Design and layout considerations

Staff need to remain vigilant during the performance of their duties. This includes:
- Being mindful of individuals showing signs of drug use
- Spotting evidence of drug paraphernalia
- Knowledge of high-risk areas such as toilets, corridors and secluded areas
- Overheard conversations involving drug references
- Following up on suspicious behaviour

Managers should be notified immediately if they suspect that any person is using, dealing, or attempting to deal drugs on the premises (whether such person is a customer or an employee of the company). All staff should also be highly aware of drink spiking being an issue in bars and clubs.

All staff are expected to fully cooperate with the authorities in any investigations arising from the use, or suspected use, of controlled drugs associated with this premises. Managers are instructed to involve the police in any case where drug dealing is involved or suspected.

In the event you make a drugs seizure, follow your company guidance (below is an example of what this guidance may look like). Always consult with the local police authority to ensure you are operating within their guidelines:

1. Ensure the process is witnessed, ideally by security or another member of staff.
2. Confiscate any drugs found, if safe to do so.
3. Record and log details of drugs found in the drug register.
4. Follow the venue procedures as laid out regarding amnesty boxes if in situ.
5. Place drugs in sealed bags (provided by police) or a sealed envelope (signed and dated across the seal).
6. Call police on the non-emergency number (101) and inform them of seizure in accordance with local police procedure. Make sure a CAD number is taken and added to the entry in the drugs register.
7. In the event of a large quantity of drugs being found, call the police (999) immediately.
8. If the drug seizure was captured on CCTV, secure backup of relevant footage.
9. Managers should be familiar with local police protocols on the seizure and holding of controlled drugs.
10. Managers should ensure they are fully trained on the use of CCTV equipment (separate CCTV policy in place to ensure correct operation).
11. Managers are required to familiarise themselves with locations of cameras and any potential "dark" spots.
12. In certain instances, it may be necessary to implement the crime scene preservation policy, for example, if there is a suspected overdose or a large quantity of controlled drug is discovered.

Disposal of Found or Seized Drugs

Only a police officer on duty is lawfully allowed to be in possession of controlled/illegal drugs. Staff and door supervisors are not authorised to possess controlled drugs.

Therefore never:
- Put drugs in your pockets
- Remove controlled substances from the premises
- Ignore drug taking
- Allow known or suspected dealers in your venue
- Act on your own – always have a witness

- Flush drugs down the toilet

If you do seize drugs, you should have an amnesty box in place which is then passed on to the authorities immediately.

Spotting the Signs of Dealing in Your Venue
- A person or group being very popular
- People taking regular trips to the toilets
- Customers staying for a short while and not buying drinks
- Secretive or sly conduct
- Known users/dealers using the venue
- Money changing hands
- Individuals with unusually large amounts of cash

Drug-Related Litter to be Vigilant for
- Syringes, pipes, tubes, scorched tinfoil, burnt spoons
- Small paper wraps, self-seal bags, small bottles, or vials
- Razor blades or plastic cards used for chopping
- Cardboard filters or hand-rolled cigarettes
- Ripped cigarette packets
- Powder on surfaces.

STAYING OPEN

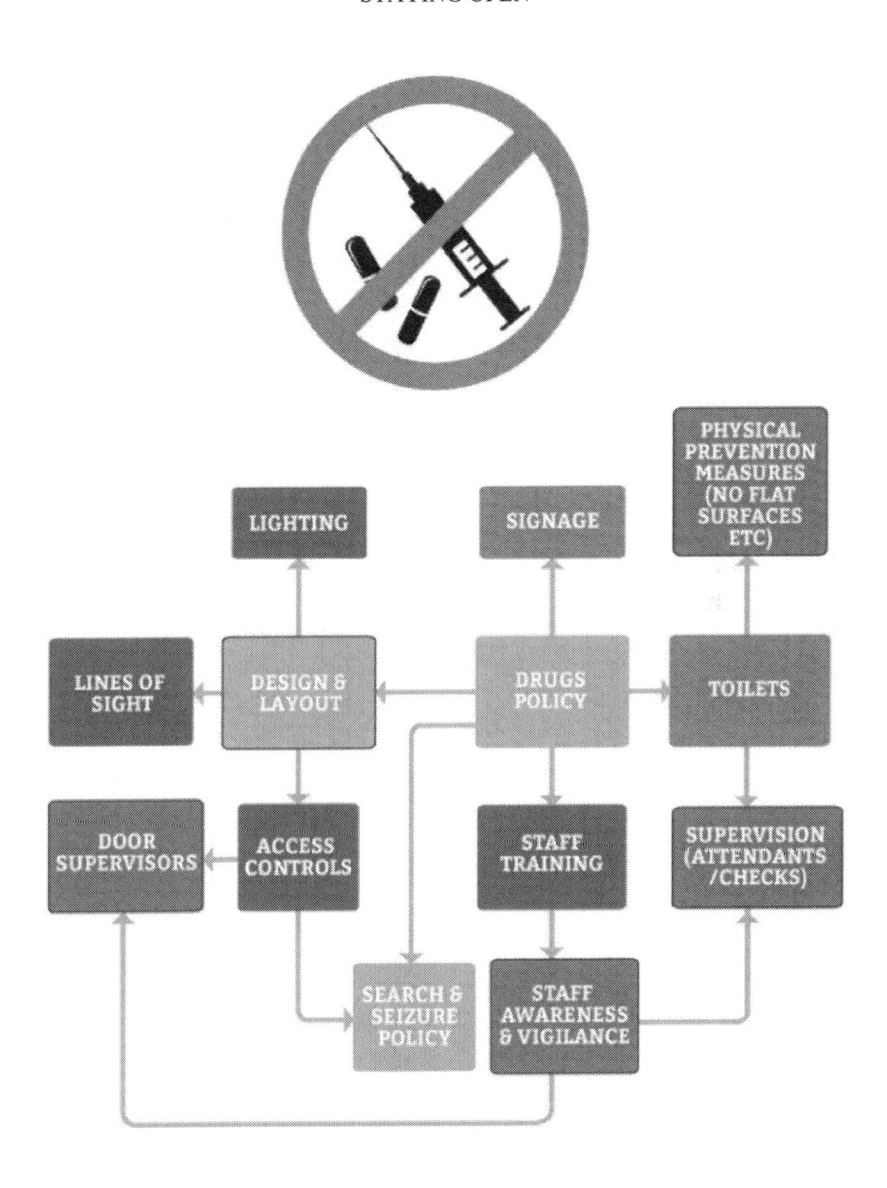

Flowchart with the following boxes and connections:

- **LIGHTING**
- **SIGNAGE**
- **PHYSICAL PREVENTION MEASURES (NO FLAT SURFACES ETC)**
- **LINES OF SIGHT**
- **DESIGN & LAYOUT**
- **DRUGS POLICY**
- **TOILETS**
- **DOOR SUPERVISORS**
- **ACCESS CONTROLS**
- **STAFF TRAINING**
- **SUPERVISION (ATTENDANTS /CHECKS)**
- **SEARCH & SEIZURE POLICY**
- **STAFF AWARENESS & VIGILANCE**

CHAPTER 9
Prevention & Intervention

"An ounce of prevention is worth a pound of cure."
- Benjamin Franklin

Police regularly scrutinise the events leading up to a serious incident. If a venue has not got the appropriate procedures and measures in place and this was a direct (or even indirect) cause of the incident (or escalation of an incident), it is likely they will take some form of remedial action.

This could range from requiring appropriate measure to be implemented to requesting conditions being added to the licence for less serious incidents; more robust action can include a review of the premises licence and even closure of the venue for more serious incidents.

The most effective incident prevention policies will combine more than one strategy at a time. For this reason, a synergistic approach combining all the three areas below will be the most effective:

1. Policies and procedures
2. Human resources
3. Physical measures

Policies & Procedures

Creating, communicating, and maintaining policies and procedures within a company is crucial to success. A typical hospitality business will have numerous policies in a variety of areas, so an efficient policy and procedure management system is critical.

A comprehensive and well-managed set of policies will be evidence of how you operate your premises within the law, promote the four licensing objectives, and provide the best possible care to guests.

The policies should form the basis of staff job descriptions, instructions, and workplace training.

Your venue should have policies and procedures for the following:
- Searching and seizure
- Age verification
- Responsible alcohol sales
- Drugs
- Guest welfare
- Ejections
- Security positions – specific job requirements
- Violence & aggression
- Management of outside/dispersal
- Smoking policy
- Incident reporting policy
- Major incident policy
- Crime scene preservation policy
- CCTV, body worn cameras, and identity scanners
- Equalities Act

Your policies and procedures must be reviewed regularly and updated as necessary. We find the best policies and procedures evolve to reflect changes to current best practices as well as learning from incidents.

Human Resources

Effective training and leadership will result in alert staff who proactively prevent incidents from occurring. As such, all staff should be trained to ensure consistency. This includes externally contracted staff such as door supervisors and toilet attendants who may be contractors. Staff need to be aware of your policies and procedures, know what to look for, and how to pro-actively assist you in managing your premises.

Things to consider:
- Staff training
- Proactive managers and staff
- Staff awareness and vigilance
- Door supervisors

- Toilet attendants
- Property patrol
- Reducing provocation through good service

Physical Measures

There is a range of physical measures that can be used to reduce opportunities for incidents to occur.

Technology is constantly improving and becoming more affordable. Cameras are smaller, have higher definition, and DVRs are smaller with huge data capacities. As such, licence conditions requiring CCTV, body worn cameras (BWC), and identity scanning are now commonplace.

The use of formal surveillance using CCTV, body worn cameras (BWC), ID Scanning equipment, and search equipment such as wands undoubtedly has an impact on preventing incidents and deterring criminals. Other technology including radios and panic alarms can also be highly effective.

But technology is not the only solution. Changing layout and increasing natural surveillance by removing obstacles to line of sight or improving lighting can have a dramatic effect on incidents at your venue.

The best form of prevention must be stopping problems coming into your premises by increasing access controls. An organised queuing system, barriers, and enclosed smoking areas will not only be effective in themselves but together with the other measures outlined, will also subconsciously inform arriving guests that your premises is organised and well-run. This will be a deterrent and affect customer behaviour.

Things to Consider:
- Design of premises (e.g. lines of sight)
- Access controls (e.g. barriers, ropes, etc.)
- Cloakroom and property control
- Searching equipment
- ID scanning equipment
- CCTV
- Body worn cameras
- Good premises maintenance
- Polycarbonate glassware
- Signage

These three important areas (policies and procedures, human resources, and physical measures) must be combined to be completely effective.

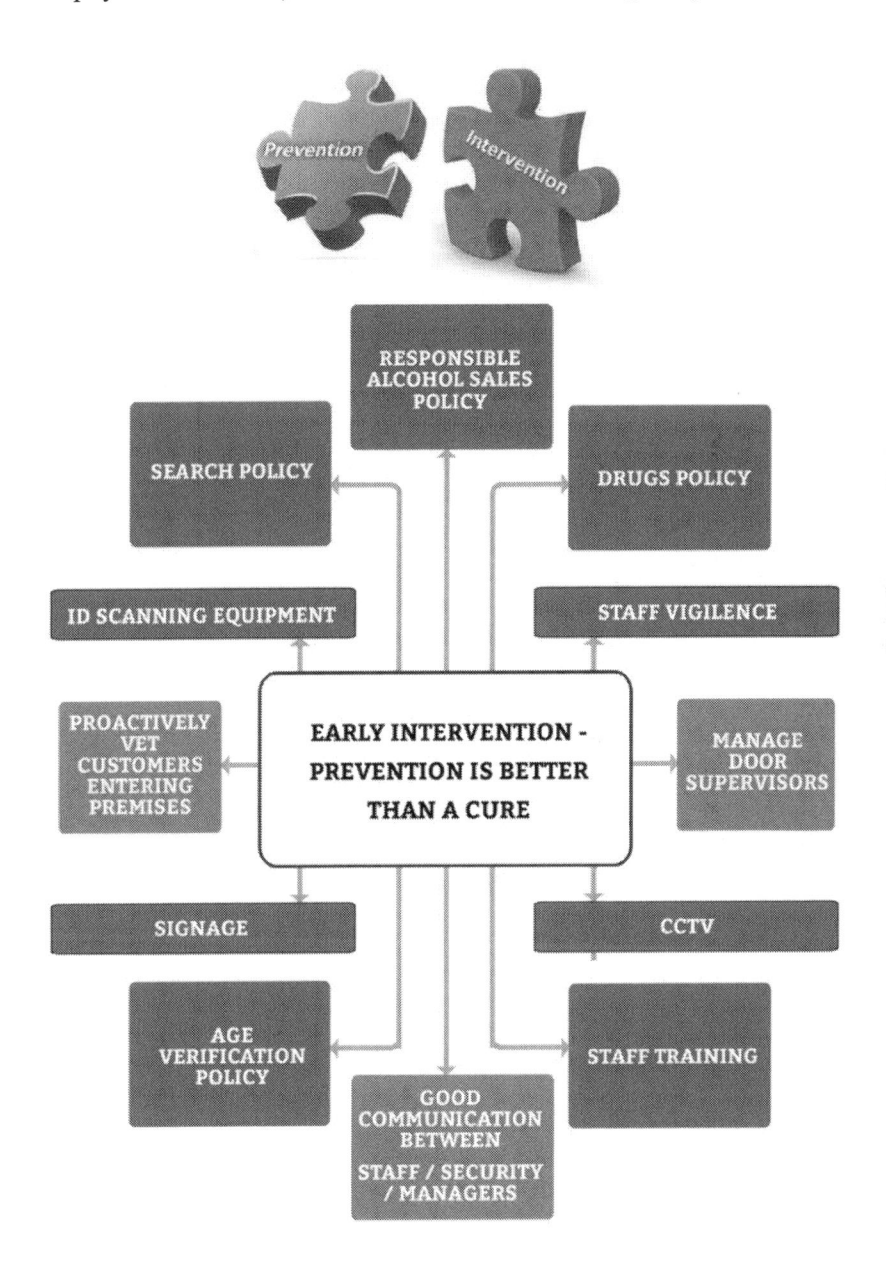

Prevention / *Intervention*

- RESPONSIBLE ALCOHOL SALES POLICY
- SEARCH POLICY
- DRUGS POLICY
- ID SCANNING EQUIPMENT
- STAFF VIGILANCE
- PROACTIVELY VET CUSTOMERS ENTERING PREMISES
- MANAGE DOOR SUPERVISORS
- SIGNAGE
- CCTV
- AGE VERIFICATION POLICY
- STAFF TRAINING
- GOOD COMMUNICATION BETWEEN STAFF / SECURITY / MANAGERS

EARLY INTERVENTION – PREVENTION IS BETTER THAN A CURE

CHAPTER 10
Door Supervisors

"Security is always excessive until it's not enough."
- Robbie Sinclair, Head of Security, Country Energy, NSW Australia

If you are the manager of a business that holds a premises licence allowing the sale of alcohol, particularly one in the late night-time economy, it is likely you will employ security; your venue may even be subject to conditions requiring minimum numbers of door supervisors. Managing a team of security can bring many challenges and it is crucial that, as a manager, you are able to supervise them properly and that they carry out their roles effectively.

Door supervisors must carry out three roles simultaneously:

Protect
Vet entry and prevent incidents

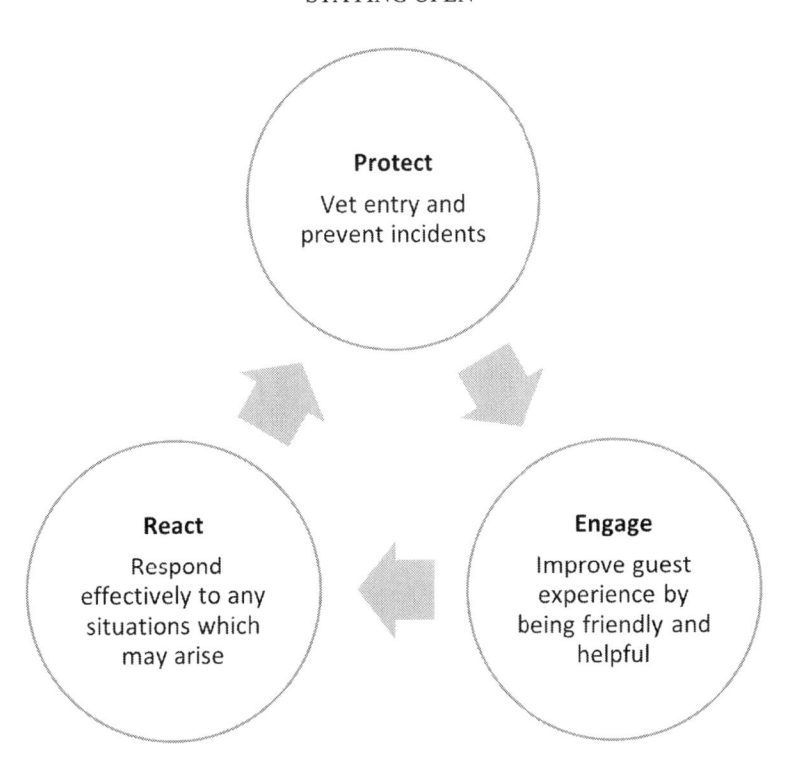

React
Respond effectively to any situations which may arise

Engage
Improve guest experience by being friendly and helpful

The action—or inaction—of the door supervisors will be seen as your success or failure by the authorities. But the ultimate responsibility of managing a security team remains with the venue management.

We often find there is real 'them' and 'us' situation where the security team is treated as a separate entity to the venue team. This can be especially prevalent when dealing with a major incident where security are left to deal with it.

But the best-run venues operate as one team with management taking the lead and security being included in briefings, training sessions, and team-building exercises.

The door supervisors are part of your core team and should be treated as such. If you are in any doubt of the impact they have on your business, both good and bad, just look at some of your online reviews. Security will most likely be the first people a guest meets when arriving at your premises. When working with venues, we often refer to door supervisors as the 'first impressions' team and the head of the security as the 'director of first impressions'. This is a different way to view the security team and the impact they can have on your business.

Background on the SIA

The Security Industry Authority (SIA) is the statutory organisation responsible for regulating the private security industry in the UK. The legislation that regulates door supervisors (and other security operatives) is the Private Security Industry Act 2001.

One of the main duties of the SIA is the compulsory licensing of individuals working in specific sectors of the private security industry. Whether or not an individual requires a licence is determined by:
- The role that is performed, and
- The activity that is undertaken

It is a criminal offence to engage in licensable conduct without a licence. If found guilty, the maximum penalty is six months imprisonment and/or an unlimited fine. The activities defined that are licensable by the Act are:
- Door Supervision (DS)
- Public Space Surveillance (CCTV)
- Security Guarding (SG)
- Key Holding (KH)
- Cash and Valuables in Transit (CVIT)
- Close Protection (CP)
- Vehicle Immobilisation (VI)

A front-line licence is required if undertaking the above licensable activities (other than key holding activities). A front-line licence is in the form of a credit card-sized plastic card that must be worn, subject to the licence conditions. This has the following information on it:
- Operatives name
- Photograph
- A 16-digit unique registration / badge number
- Expiry date

Public Space Surveillance (CCTV)

It is important to note a separate Public Space Surveillance (CCTV) licence is required when manned guarding activities are carried out through the use of closed circuit television equipment to:

1. Monitor the activities of a member of the public in a public or private place; or
2. Identify a particular person.

Licensing Act 2003

All premises licences which authorise the supply of alcohol are subject to the same mandatory conditions. One of which relates to door supervisors and is worded as follows:

"All persons guarding premises against unauthorised access or occupation or against outbreaks of disorder or against damage (door supervisors) must be licensed by the Security Industry Authority."

The Four Licensing Objectives

As you know you have a duty to promote the Four Licensing Objectives.
1. The prevention of crime and disorder
2. Public safety
3. The prevention of public nuisance
4. The protection of children from harm

Effective use of door supervisors can promote all four of the objectives.

Venue Specific Licence Conditions

Many premises will also be subject to conditions on their premises licence regarding the provision of door supervisors. They may include:

- Minimum numbers of door supervisors
- Door supervisors in certain roles or positions
- Details of door supervisors to be recorded
- That they wear high visibility clothing

Common Mistakes

1. Security running the venue
It is common for security, normally the head of security, to fill any gaps in the management of a premises. Security teams work best when there is strong leadership from venue management.

2. Processes breaking down when there is a lack of communication
It is crucial the team communicate effectively with one another and venue management.

3. Allowing standards to slip
Keep on top of the small details and you will be in a much stronger position.

4. Not showing your appreciation!
If a security team feels undervalued and unappreciated, morale will drop and the team will not perform well.

Tips on managing the security team
- Think of the security as part of your team – include them in staff training sessions and briefings (where appropriate).
- Monitor their performance and interactions.
- Ensure you offer additional training including radio etiquette.
- Meet with the areas managers of the contracting company regularly.
- Don't ignore issues (even minor ones) – take action and prevent a situation escalating.
- Be realistic in your expectations – often we find the security operatives are among the lowest paid staff on the premises yet often the most is expected of them.

Security Induction Training
Before commencement of first shift, induction training is carried out as follows:

- All staff are inducted as close to the commencement of employment as possible
- All staff briefed on emergency action plans
- All staff briefed on SOPs
- All staff are given a walk around of the site they are deployed at prior to commencing their first shift
- Emergency procedures and walkthrough of emergency exits is carried out at the same time
- The Code of Conduct Signed before commencing work

Commencing the Shift

Upon arrival at the site each shift, door supervisors must ensure they:
- Sign in for duty with name, badge number, and expiry date recorded
- Report to the duty manager to receive information on any plans, problems, or concerns
- Collect two-way radios and Body Worn Cameras – sign these in and out
- Ensure their SIA card is always worn and visible while on site

At the end of each shift and before they leave the premises, the operatives must ensure that:
- All observations and incidents have been logged in the security logbook
- Two-way radios and Body Worn Cameras (if relevant) are collected, switched off, and placed in the charger
- Sign off in the shift logbook

Delivering Excellent Service

You want to give your guest the best experience possible and provide a high level of customer service by ensuring that your door supervisors are:
- Smiling and welcoming
- Remaining professional in their appearance
- Treating visitors with respect
- Being positive at all times
- Maintaining friendly eye contact
- Being interested in what the guest has to say
- Being observant at all times
- Being proactive

Security Logbook

All observations and incidents should be recorded in the security logbook. An incident report must be completed for serious incidents – defined as any incident requiring the submission of an incident report or where emergency services such as police have been contacted. We always recommend that managers complete an incident report for serious incidents.

We provide our clients with our record-keeping system called the One Day Record. This is a coding system for security staff that is easy to use and saves time during shifts. An online version is available through our website.

What to do in the following circumstances

Most managers assume that each door supervisor will know what to do in a myriad of circumstances - do not assume this is the case. If someone can get something wrong, they usually will.

Create a matrix of likely and possible scenarios and give clear guidance on who must be alerted and what action must be taken. Here is a template you can use:

Circumstance	Who to Alert	Course of Action
THEFT		
DRUG DEALING		
AGGRESSION & VIOLENCE		
CRIME SCENE PRESERVATION		
TERROR ATTACK		
INTOXICATION		
ACCIDENT		
FIRE		

Things Your Security Team Should NOT Do

- Use a mobile phone whilst on duty for private calls
- Use any device to listen to music via headphones whilst on duty
- Lean on walls, railings, or sit down
- Act in a rude or disrespectful manner to any visitor or team

member
- Handle cash in any way such as out of registers, from customers, or in transit to or from the admin office
- Handle cigarettes
- Store personal bags, wallets, or items on their person
- Receive deliveries
- Read newspapers, magazines, or any other reading material whilst on duty
- Behave in a manner that endangers a person's safety
- Put themselves, customers, or team members in a threatening situation
- Leave their position or the venue without telling anyone

De-Escalation is Key

Remember your conflict management training. Prevention and de-escalation are always at the top of the list of actions to take when appropriate. Our RASPFLO™ Managers course has a useful section on conflict management.

Preventing Positional Asphyxia

In light of the tragic death of George Floyd in Minneapolis, we have included an additional section the end of the book on awareness of how to prevent positional asphyxia.

In short, be aware that is a global issue and not restricted to police forces. Never restrain anyone on the ground. Get the person onto their feet as soon as possible and always make sure that they can breathe.

Assessing Security Requirements

It is critical that you correctly assess your business' security requirements. There are several factors that must be considered to ensure that you have the appropriate level of security.

Capacity of Venue

Many people, including some enforcement officers, cite the old "1 security to every 100 guests" rule for calculating minimum numbers. In fact, this is incorrect; the original formula was 2 security for the first 100 guests and then 1 security for every 100 guests thereafter. However, as you can see by the factors below, this is not a reliable or effective way of assessing the numbers of security your premises may need.

Location of Venue
There is a world of difference between a venue in a quiet, rural setting and one on a busy high street in a city centre. The location of your venue may mean that your security team must deal with lots of issues outside the premises. It may also have an impact on the profile of your guests.

Layout of Venue
A venue on multiple levels may need more security than a premises on one level. Lines of sight, numbers of exits, and travel times will also impact on the positions you should cover.

Operating Times
The risk of aggression and violence increases exponentially each hour after midnight. If you are trading until 6am, it may be sensible to have more security than if you were trading until 3am.

Activity
Some activities will be higher risk than others. For example, a Northern soul or jazz all-nighter is likely less problematic than a techno all-nighter. Different activities will attract different issues, and some music genres may mean a greater likelihood of drugs, or violence. You may need to allocate more security to vetting entry, searching, controlling queues, or patrolling inside the premises.

Customer Profile
Your customer profile will also have an impact on security requirements. An older demographic is less likely to bring issues of aggression, violence, drugs, and drunkenness. Events promoted to a younger audience are likely to attract underage people, meaning you will need to direct more resources to age checks.

Previous Incidents
Consider the history of the premises, even a particular event's previous incidents. An event which has had problems in the past may require more security.

Team Structure
As part of your security assessment, you will have identified specific roles and positions requirements for security. It is important that the right operative is employed for each task and provided with the correct information to carry out that role. A good example of a security team would be comprised of the following:

Head of Security
This is clearly the key role and it is essential you have the right person for the role. The head of security is normally positioned on the door.

Deputy Head of Security
It is important the deputy can step up if the HoS is absent. They will normally be positioned inside managing internal security.

Roaming Security
Patrolling the venue, responding to calls, and handling ejections.

Vetting Security
Assessing suitability, age and ID checks, and searching. Security employed to vet entry must be provided with the following information:
- The terms of entry (e.g. dress code)
- Age restrictions (e.g. no under 18s)
- Searching requirements (e.g. physical searches, bags only, metal detecting wands)
- ID scanning

The above points may be compulsory by licence condition. If this is the case, the terms of the condition must be clearly explained to the operative.

Static Positions
Key positions throughout the venue, including pinch and flashpoints, fire exits, etc.

Marshalling
Arrivals, queues, dispersal.

Some door supervisors will have a natural aptitude for certain tasks, and it is important that you recognise and utilise these traits. For example, a very sociable, outgoing person will be more suitable for interacting with guests on the front door. Some operatives will not work as well in a static position, preferring a more active role. It is also good practice to rotate positions to avoid complacency and to keep the team alert.

Communication
Good and effective communication is crucial for the management of your

premises and your security team. Accurate information needs to be passed quickly to the right people.

Chain of Command
Each member of security must know who is in charge and who has key roles within the operation. They need to understand where information should be passed at the appropriate time.

Radios
All the security should understand basic radio etiquette. This will include no unnecessary chatter and keeping transmissions short, clear, and to the point.

It is extremely important there is a proper protocol for radio use, especially in a nightclub environment. It is this protocol, along with good situational awareness, that can help prevent serious incidents.

Radios allow an open, clear line of communication that is essential in any environment where one needs to transmit information over large distances or where an individual is not within the sight line of another individual. Radios allow security, staff and management to keep tabs on each other, warn one another of potentially dangerous situations, and exchange important information.

Security (and all staff using radios) must understand basic rules for radio use:
- Consistency is important! Everyone communicating in the same way reduces mistakes. That means everyone using the same codes in the same manner.
- Pay attention. Just because your name or location wasn't mentioned DOES NOT mean that the communication isn't important to you. The message may indicate special instructions needed in your area.
- Avoid stepping on other transmissions. Allow the speaker(s) to finish their transmission before speaking.

Channel Use
- Depending on the size of your venue, each department/section/job should have their own designated Channel. Example below:
- Channel 1 – Security
- Channel 2 – Front of House (Management/Hostess)

STAYING OPEN

- Channel 3 – Bar/Floor Staff

This cuts down on radio interference and chatter and makes it easy for people to switch back and forth depending on who they need to talk to.

Radio Silence
Good radio etiquette demands that all users limit their communication to essential radio calls only. Unless you have something important to say – don't talk. That means no idle chit chat.

How to Speak
Hold down the transmit button for one or two seconds before talking. Most radios will cut you off if you begin to speak immediately. When you do speak, keep your messages brief and to the point. For one, it lessens the chances that someone will misunderstand what you are saying; second, it keeps conversation to the bare minimum.
1. Announce yourself – state your name and then the name of the person to whom you are directing your call (i.e. "Tom for Jerry.")
2. Wait for acknowledgement – "Go ahead Tom."…and then state your message.

Radio Codes/Slang
Team members should be informed of any radio codes and when to use them. Each premises will have developed its own codes (for example, code red = violence, code blue = visit from authorities/police etc.).

Note that the codes may not be the same everywhere, so it is important new security know the codes for your premises.

In stressful situations, it is difficult for individuals to remember a list of codes for different types of emergencies in different locations unless they have been trained regularly in the use of these codes.

But there are some basics that can save you trouble or misunderstanding:
- Abort – stop what you are doing or disregard that last transmission
- Affirmative/Negative – yes or no
- Over – I've finished talking: "Do you need the chair in VIP? Over."
- Out – I've finished talking and don't expect a reply: "I will take care of that immediately. Out."

- Go Ahead – send your transmission: "This is Tom, go ahead."
- Say Again – repeat your message: "Say again, Tom."
- Copy/Roger – helps the transmitter know that someone got their message: "Tom, bring the trashcan to the 2nd floor." "Copy that.")

Words to Avoid
- Oops
- What, Huh?
- Yep, yeah
- Oh, God!
- Wait a sec…
- Are you there?
- Got it

The main reason to avoid these is that they serve no purpose whatsoever. Again, do not waste airspace.

In Case of Emergency
Keep the transmissions short and to the point. It is also especially important to not yell out what the emergency is to avoid what could be a possible panic situation (i.e. a fire).

If you are dealing with an out of control altercation or are in immediate physical danger, the easiest way to ask for assistance is to announce your location 3 TIMES ("Dance Floor! Dance Floor! Dance Floor!"). This tells everyone where they need to head.

Radios are one of the most useful tools for the security team. Train your team how and when to use them and make sure that everyone knows the rules of use before they begin wearing a radio. If necessary, correct improper usage (recommended after a shift) and teach your team the radio etiquette that will work best for your venue.

Outside/Inside
It is incredibly important that the left hand knows what the right hand is doing. If something occurs inside it could have a great impact on the outside and vice versa. The security needs to understand that the appropriate information is passed between the two parties. For example, if a guest is being ejected, security at the entrance should be informed so they can clear the way.

Conclusion

Your security team is your front-line defence, the guards at the door, protecting you, your staff, your guests, your property and, indeed, your business. They form a critical part of your business. It is in everyone's interest that they are effective and perform their role well.

CHAPTER 11
Events & Private Hire

"Be proactive not reactive, for an apparently insignificant issue ignored today can spawn tomorrow's catastrophe."

- Ken Poirot

Imagine hosting an event that was initially described as a birthday party. But it turns out to be a large, promoted event that escalates into serious issues. The venue is at maximum capacity, there is a large queue of impatient guests, and police end up being called to break up a fight. If you had been given proper knowledge of the type of event it was, you would not have booked it under any circumstances.

The point being that something perceived to be inconsequential can end up having terrible consequences.

In the same way that you would vet people wishing to enter your premises, you should also thoroughly vet any person who would like to hold an event at your premises. To do this, implement a booking and events policy to ensure all events have been risk assessed, are right for your venue, and have the appropriate and proportionate measures and resources allocated to it.

All private bookings and events held at your venue should be subject to rigorous vetting, and any booking should not be confirmed without the approval of the Designated Premises Supervisor (DPS).

Anyone wishing to book a private party should be required to attend the premises in person to meet with management (unless they are already known to management). No bookings should be taken solely over the telephone or by email.

If you don't already, implement a booking form – any person wishing to book a private party will be required to provide the following information that will be recorded:
- The nature of the event (e.g. corporate event, launch party, etc.)
- The numbers invited
- The style of music to be played
- A full guest list prior to the event
- The name, date of birth, home address, email address, and telephone number of the organiser (photographic ID to be supplied)
- The name, date of birth, home address and telephone number of any DJ's playing at the private party
- Whether tickets are being sold
- A copy of the invitation prior to the event
- Full details of any outside promoters

You can get a detailed risk assessment checklist on our website.

Each event should be risk assessed individually and the appropriate numbers of registered door supervisors employed. Part of your assessment may include contacting venues that have held previous events by the organiser.

Persons holding the event will be informed that:
- The event will be held subject to risk assessment
- An invitation does not guarantee entry – all persons will be vetted on the door
- All guests may be subject to a search
- The premises operates a strict policy on drugs and weapons – any person found in possession of either will be detained and reported to the police immediately

Events should be monitored throughout and, if you feel appropriate, stopped at any time.

It is also good practice to retain your booking form as a record of each event with a note of any issues you experienced.

CHAPTER 12
Management of Outside Area & Dispersal

"If a man loudly blesses his neighbour early in the morning, it will be taken as a curse."
- Proverbs 27:14

Nuisance is a common issue faced by late night venues. The most common are music noise and customer noise outside the premises. But odours, litter, and antisocial behaviour are also considered a nuisance.

Many late licensed venues' premises licences carry standard conditions preventing nuisance. As such, local residents who experience nuisance are in a position to take action against that venue. The Prevention of Public Nuisance is a licensing objective and, therefore, a valid reason to bring a review of the premises licence. You could also be subject to a noise abatement notice if causing a nuisance is established by council officers.

It is essential that any late licensed premises has a strategy for managing customers outside the venue. Procedures should be designed to ensure there is an absolute minimum of noise and to prevent any nuisance being caused to neighbours and the general public.

A robust policy will consider the following measures:
1. Roles and responsibilities
2. Entry controls
3. During trading
4. Guests smoking
5. Exit controls
6. Other measures
7. Complaints procedure and contacts

Roles and Responsibilities

Your policy should lay out who is responsible for implementing the policy and the roles of those who will carry it out. Have daily briefings that identify any specific issues (e.g. events or bookings) that may have an impact on management of the policy. Briefings should also cover learning and feedback from any previous incidents or events held.

It is also important that all staff are trained in procedures so they know their responsibilities and receive regular refresher training.

Entry Controls

As we discussed in the Prevention and Intervention chapter, an organised queuing system, barriers, and enclosed smoking areas will subconsciously inform arriving guests that your premises is organised and well-run. Thus, helping to create a positive atmosphere and reduce nuisance.

Even so, any guests queuing outside your venue have the potential to cause a nuisance, whether from noise or simply obstructing the roads. Here are some simple measures to avoid nuisance before entry:

- Queues should always be managed by door supervisors and marshals
- Guests should be advised of waiting times
- Those that will not be admitted should be told before they reach the head of the queue

During Trading

Managers and security should monitor activity outside throughout trading hours, particularly guests temporarily leaving the premises to smoke or use their telephone.

Any illegal activity which could give rise to nuisance, such as flower sellers and taxi touts who will often target your guests should be discouraged by security.

Guests Smoking

You should develop a separate smoking policy so staff understand how to manage smokers. There may be conditions on your licence restricting where guests can smoke and even maximum numbers of smokers at any one time so ensure these factors are included in your policy and understood by all staff.

Exit Controls

Closing time (when guests leave your premises) is critical when it comes to preventing noise and nuisance. You should always endeavour to create a slow stream of guests leaving to prevent large groups congregating outside your premises.

Door supervisors should be proactive about dispersal of groups and encourage guests to leave the area quickly and quietly. As guests leave and your premises empties, door supervisors from inside the venue should be posted outside to assist with dispersal.

Other Measures

There are several other measures you can implement that will have a positive impact on reducing the potential for noise and nuisance:
- Slow the tempo and lower the volume of music inside the premises at the end of the night so guests are calmer and less noisy as they leave.
- Raise the house lights gradually to ease guests in the transition from partying to going home.
- Make sure information is available to guests on transport links so they can get home easily (some venues even add the location of car parks in the area and other travel facilities on promotional materials).
- Prominently display notices at exits politely requesting guests to respect the needs of local residents.

Remember, your staff can also contribute to nuisance. Ensure that staff who arrive early in the morning or depart late at night are instructed to avoid causing disturbance or nuisance to nearby residents.

Finally, make sure the areas outside your venue are swept. Litter such as cigarette butts, flyers, bottles, etc. are a common cause of complaint from residents.

Complaints Procedure and Contacts

Provide a telephone number to local residents for them to call should they have an issue. After all, it's much better if they complain to you rather than the authorities. You'll then be able to take remedial action and solve the problem which is far better than facing enforcement action.

If you do receive a complaint, it should be dealt with promptly by a senior member of staff on duty. The complaint should also be reviewed and followed up by the Designated Premises Supervisor (DPS) the next working day.

A detailed record must be kept of any complaint received. This will include the nature of the complaint and action taken together with the details of the complainant.

Finally, your entire policy should be reviewed on an annual basis at minimum to ensure its effectiveness and relevance is not compromised
.

CHAPTER 13
CCTV, Body Worn Cameras (BWC), & Identity Scanners

"Our society is not one of spectacle but of surveillance."
- Michel Foucault

There is no doubt that CCTV is ubiquitous in society and increasingly so in licensed premises. It is a primary element in the prevention of crime and disorder and it can have huge evidential value in prosecuting offenders. Police will generally always ask for comprehensive CCTV systems to be installed in late licensed premises and CCTV conditions are commonplace on premises licences. Body Worn Cameras (BWC) are a relatively new product that are now being used far more widely in recent years.

It's crucial that CCTV and BWC are operated effectively and in line with the Data Protection Act 1998 and The General Data Protection Regulation 2016/679 (GDPR). Licensed premises should be able to demonstrate that their CCTV system is working, has been operational historically, and that any issues are resolved as soon as possible. We recommend policy and procedures are developed to ensure your business meets these standards.

Most police licensing officers will ask that premises, at a minimum, has one camera that shows a close-up at the entrance to capture a clear, head and shoulders identifying image of every person entering. Persons entering your premises should be asked to remove any headwear which obscures their faces unless it is worn as part of religious observance.

The system should record in real-time and recordings must be date and time stamped – these will need to be made available to police or the licensing authority upon request as soon as possible. Recordings should then be maintained for a minimum of a month (but check your premises licence as you may have a licence condition that specifies the number of days recordings should be kept on file).

Your CCTV system should always be kept secure, with access limited to the DPS and managers. You should also keep a dedicated CCTV system log. All usage, checks, faults, and requests for images will be recorded in the log. Any person taking a copy of the CCTV such as the police, fire authority or local authority officer must sign in the relevant section of the log acknowledging receipt of the data. The signing officer should also enter their place of work and a contact telephone number.

A full incident report should be made of any faults with the system. When reporting any faults with the CCTV system, include anticipated times scales for repairs and who the issue has been escalated to if these time scales are not met.

The DPS and all managers should be trained in the use of the CCTV system. The training should include interrogation of the system and transfer of images to separate media (CD, DVD, flash drive etc.).

Ensure there is always at least one person who is suitably trained and conversant with the CCTV system on the premises when open to the public. This is often a licence condition.

We recommend a weekly documented test is carried out to ensure the system is working correctly. A record of these checks showing the date and name of the person checking should be kept as part of your due diligence evidence.

Signage should be placed prominently at the entrance to your venue advising all persons entering that CCTV is in operation in accordance with the Data Protection Act 1998 and GDPR. The notice should clearly state the name of the Data Controller, the purpose of the CCTV (e.g. prevention and detection of crime, public and employee safety, etc.) and contact details for subject access.

Body Worn Cameras (BWC)

BWCs can be an excellent tool in terms of evidence and investigating incidents. They can also be a deterrent and protect your staff. The added advantages over fixed CCTV are that you have audio and can follow events around your premises.

The use of BWCs should only ever be:
- Proportionate
- Legitimate
- Necessary
- Justifiable

BWCs are capable of capturing primary evidence that gives a compelling and indisputable account of the circumstances. This doesn't replace the need to capture other types of evidence but will go a considerable way in reducing any ambiguities and should be considered as an additional security aid.

You need to ensure that the use of BWCs is dealt with within any training you provide to the security team. A lack of proper training will inevitably mean that the use of BWCs is not effective.

Door supervisors should 'book out' their BWC and the details logged so you know who had which camera and to prevent loss of equipment.

Before use, check each device is charged and all previously captured images and audio is removed prior to deployment. The device should be fixed to the door supervisors (or operative's) outer clothing where the field of view is clear and not obscured.

BWC video footage must be held in compliance with the Data Protection Act and GDPR requirements. Footage should be held for a specific period (e.g. 31 days) unless there is a need for it to be held longer (i.e. as evidence of a crime). We recommend adding the fact that BWCs are in use to your CCTV signage.

As with CCTV recordings, BWC footage should be provided to police upon request with the absolute minimum of delay. We recommend that door supervisors, where possible, record any physical ejections and any incidents of crime and/or disorder for this purpose.

Identity Scanning Systems

The use of identity scanning systems in late licensed premises is becoming more and more common. They are favoured by police who see

them as an excellent tool for:
- Deterring criminals and antisocial behaviour
- Providing suspect and witness identities in the event of a serious incident
- Enabling licensed premises to exchange information about customers who have caused problems in venues

In fact, many premises now have a licence condition requiring the use of an identity scanning system as a condition of entry.

As identity scanning systems hold personal data, they must conform with the requirements of the Data Protection Act 1998 and GDPR and follow the Information Commissioner's Office Good Practice advice.

The only forms of identification accepted for use with the ID scanner are:
- A passport
- National identity card
- Photographic driving licence
- A PASS approved proof of age card
- An armed forces identity card

Signage

Signs should be prominently displayed at the entrance of your premises which explain why the ID system is in operation. The notice will also explain to customers that providing satisfactory identification to be electronically scanned and recorded is a condition of entry. It is good practice to also display your Privacy Policy.

Sharing Information

Only a manager should decide whether information should be shared with other venues on the identity scanning system in the interest of public safety or prevention of crime.

You should not use or share customers' personal information for marketing or commercial activity unless they have 'opted in' for such use. However, personal information can be shared with police or other enforcement agencies investigating crimes upon request.

Ensure that only relevant information is scanned for the purposes of confirming and recording the identity of customers.

Access to Personal Information

Access to scanning system records must be restricted to those whose duties require it. Only managers should be able to access all record fields including addresses on the identity scanning system.

If the data is stored and encrypted locally on the HDD of a computer, it must be kept securely with only managers able to access the data. The data on the computer should be password protected and staff with authority have individual usernames and passwords which will allow a record or log of any person accessing personal data. You also need to consider the location of screens and what information is displayed to the public when scanning takes place.

The ID scanning equipment has a transactional logging and audit capability to allow regular security reviews to counter any possible system abuse.

Data Retention

You should only keep records for as long as there is a reasonable requirement to do so. For example, any details relating to a customer who has not visited your premises over a year will be deleted unless there is a serious reason to not do so.

Alternatively, your policy may be that data is retained for a minimum of six months and reviewed annually when senior management will conduct a purge of data.

Subject Access

People have a right to view personal data held about them; this is called subject access. Individuals may request copies of the personal information held on the identity scanning machine using subject access procedures. Any request to delete personal data should be considered and decided by senior management.

Maintenance

Your identity scanning system should be kept in good working order and any faults or operating issues be fully incident reported.

Data Protection

The GDPR places requirements on business handling personal data.

These include carrying out a data impact assessment and creating a privacy policy. This applies to the use of CCTV, identity scanners, and BWCs.

Further information is available from the Information Commissioner's Office (ICO).

CHAPTER 14
Record Keeping

"Diligence is the mother of good fortune."
- Benjamin Disraeli

When an incident happens, you need to show you took all reasonable precautions and exercised all due diligence in the management of your premises. Comprehensive records demonstrate responsible and proactive management and can protect you against allegations of poor operations offences. They are also an excellent management tool enabling you to measure the effectiveness of your business and compliance regime.

The Licensing Act contains a number of offences that allow a defence of 'due diligence'. These include (among others):
- Selling alcohol to someone under the age of 18 years old
- Carrying on or attempting to carry on an unauthorised licensable activities
- Exposing alcohol for unauthorised sale
- Keeping alcohol on the premises for unauthorised sale

Due diligence is, therefore, very important and it may be what you rely on if something goes wrong in the future. Even though licensing law is absolute, keeping comprehensive records will always be helpful if you do need to rely on them.

So, What is Due Diligence?
In brief, due diligence can be defined as the ability to show that all reasonable steps to avoid committing the offence were taken. There are two parts to this defence, and they are defined in the Licensing Act as follows:

1. The act was due to a mistake, or to reliance on information given, or loan act or omission by another person, or to some other cause beyond their control, and
2. They took all reasonable precautions and exercised all due diligence.

Here is a useful list of the various records you can keep with examples given for each:

Pre-Opening Safety Checks

Pre-opening safety check records provide important evidence that emergency exits, lighting, signage, and fire safety equipment are all maintained, working, and in place.

For example, during a statutory authority inspection, it is discovered a fire exit is obstructed. The manager can prove the exit was checked and was free of obstruction earlier in the evening.

Clicker Counts/Accommodation Numbers

Recording clicker counts shows that a safe capacity is managed and never exceeded.

For example, if a customer complains to the licensing authority that your premises was overcrowded on a particular night, the manager can provide detailed records of numbers in the premises at the relevant time to refute the allegation.

Refusal of Entry

Recording any refusals of entry demonstrates customers are vetted before being allowed entry and that you do not just have an open-door policy.

For example, if there was an allegation that you allow anyone into your premises, a record of refusals is evidence that there is an entry policy and unsuitable people are refused entry.

Refusal of Service

Recording refusals of service show that you do not serve intoxicated or underage persons.

For example, if an allegation is made that you served an underaged person, a record of refusals is evidence that customers are assessed by staff before being served.

Ejections

Recording ejections shows that any unsuitable guests (e.g. through intoxication, behaviour etc.) are asked to leave the premises.

For example, if there is an allegation that you run a 'disorderly house', a record of any ejections demonstrates you are proactive in patrolling your venue. A record of all ejections can also be useful if a customer alleges unnecessary force was used.

Door Supervisor Log

Keeping a door supervisor log shows you check that only properly SIA registered staff with valid badges are employed at your premises.

For example, if there was an allegation that you do not have SIA registered staff or that you do not employ enough security, a record of your SIA staff can demonstrate that you do use correctly licensed staff. It can also identify which staff were working on a particular night if police are investigating an incident.

Toilet Checks

Recording toilet checks demonstrates that toilets are regularly checked for the welfare of your guests and criminal activity.

For example, if there was an allegation that customers were using toilets to do drugs, toilet records are evidence that this area is supervised and regularly patrolled.

CCTV Checks

Documented CCTV checks can be used as evidence your CCTV is working correctly and holds footage for the minimum requirement of 31 days.

For example, you may have a licence condition that your CCTV should be maintained to a minimum standard and have images for 31 days. If there was an incident and police required footage, but you attempt to download the footage and find the system has failed and the images are not there, your licence would be vulnerable because the condition was not met. Regular, recorded CCTV checks can demonstrate that the system was working correctly during the last test.

Incident Reports

A good incident report ensures details of any incident is recorded at the time, should there be a requirement for investigation at a later date.

For example, an allegation is made that your premises failed to deal with a serious incident properly. The manager's incident report shows that the correct steps were taken.

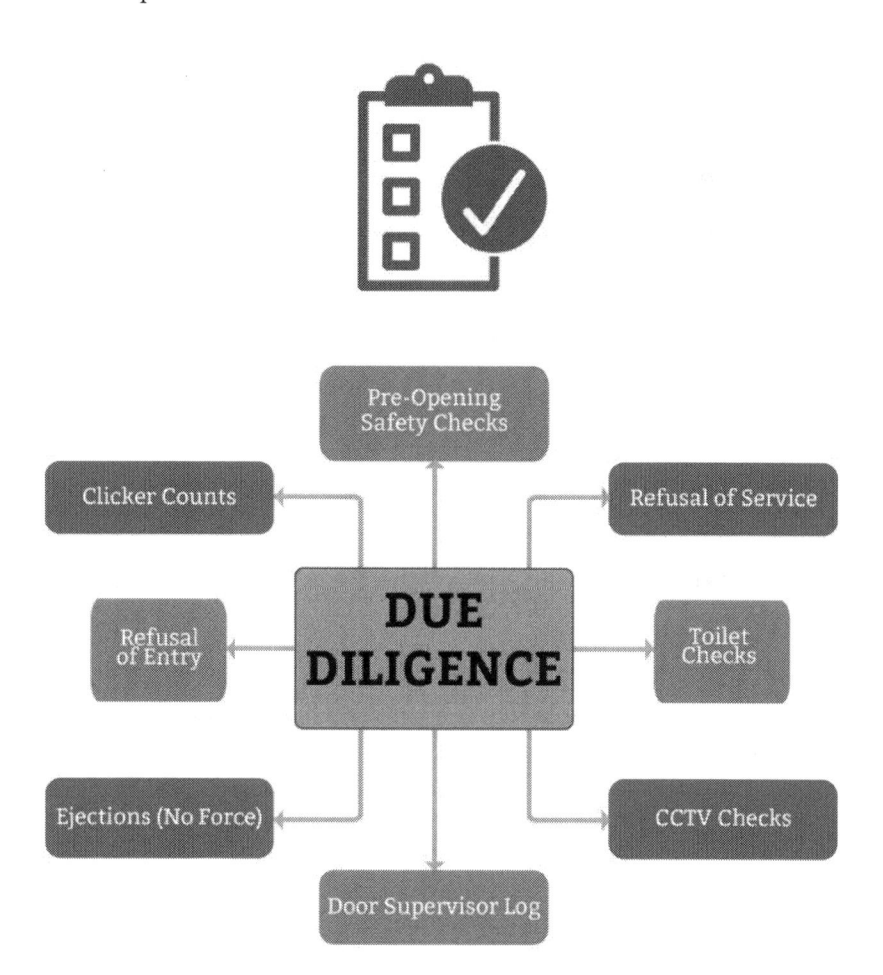

DUE DILIGENCE
- Pre-Opening Safety Checks
- Clicker Counts
- Refusal of Service
- Refusal of Entry
- Toilet Checks
- Ejections (No Force)
- CCTV Checks
- Door Supervisor Log

SECTION 3
If the Worst Happens: Reactive Measures

CHAPTER 15
Guest Welfare

"It is not enough to be compassionate. You must act."
- Dalai Lama

This chapter aims to provide those working in the licensed industry with an awareness of vulnerability and their responsibilities towards people visiting their premises.

This has become a major area of focus in recent times. The Metropolitan Police introduced the WAVE (Welfare and Vulnerability Engagement) training in 2018 to provide those working in the licensed industry with an awareness of vulnerability and their responsibilities towards people visiting their premises.

There is a clear responsibility for operators to have a duty of care for their customers. You have a social, legal, and moral responsibility towards them. Aside from this, the vast majority of businesses want their guests to have a good time in a safe environment.

To put this in perspective, a young female guest was removed from a West End club and later run over and killed by two taxis. In another tragic incident in Portsmouth, a removed guest drowned in the Solent. Because of avoidable cases such as these, the police have upped the ante in this area to ensure vulnerable guests are kept safe.

Early intervention is always is key. All staff, including door supervisors, already play an important role in protecting vulnerable guests. Building on experience and sharing knowledge with all staff will help spot early signs of vulnerability.

All staff should have the ability to recognise vulnerable people and make interventions that will reduce the risk of harm to that person. This doesn't negate the need for people to look after themselves and act responsibly, but there will be occasions when people don't recognise the risk they face.

There are various policies and procedures – both from a licensing and a health & safety perspective – that address the welfare of guests:
- Risk assessments
- First aiders
- A responsible alcohol sales policy
- Door supervisors, etc.

There are two main factors vulnerable people—particularly through intoxication, drug use, or a drink being spiked—are far more susceptible to:

1. **Becoming the victim of crime:**
   - They are less aware of their property and can become the victim of theft
   - They are less aware of their surroundings and can become victims of assault (e.g. knocking into people, sitting at the wrong table, spilling drinks and prompting an aggressive response from other people).
   - They are less aware of their surroundings and can become a victim of sexual assault (including a Drug Facilitated Sexual Assault [DFSA], drink spiking, or date rape).
2. **Having an accident:**
   - Slips, trips, or a fall
   - Road traffic accidents

The WAVE training course developed by the Metropolitan police is excellent and all front of house staff should undertake it. You can contact the police directly or we can deliver this training for you.

STAYING OPEN

> The police have a free resource on their website to assist you with training. They also have some excellent training films that are freely available to download along with course materials:
>
> **https://nbcc.police.uk/guidance/wave-presentation**
>
> For those premises pressed for time or who are looking for additional insights, we can deliver this course for them. Details are on our website.

In late-2019, we dealt with a premises review. Near the top of the review was a failure of the premises to conduct WAVE training as one of the reasons for the review to take place. So, this is a vital part of your policies that should not be overlooked.

What is the Benefit of Adopting WAVE in Your Premises?
- Provide a safer environment for the guests
- Reduce crime on the premises
- Reduce the chance of a sexual assault taking place
- Decrease the chances of a guest coming to harm either on or off the premises
- Increase guest satisfaction
- Improve working partnerships with statutory authorities
- Enhance staff training
- Lower instances of ASB (Anti-Social Behaviour).
- Prevent/reduce sexual offences
- Reduce preventable injury linked to alcohol and drug use in the licensed economy
- Reduce opportunities for criminal activity and anti-social behaviour in licensed premises
- Promote partnerships and engagement with communities and key stakeholders in the licensed economy

WAVE initiatives help to identify people before they become potentially vulnerable, as well as:
- Victims of crime
- Victims of anti-social behaviour
- Those who have come to harm in any other way
- Those involved in crime/antisocial behaviour/harm

It also aims to ensure vulnerable people are properly supported with positive interventions. Ultimately, WAVE is a prevention and harm reduction initiative.

But What is Vulnerability?

There are several ways of defining vulnerability but for the purpose of this book, we will use the following broad definition taken from the Oxford English Dictionary:

> Anyone exposed to the possibility of being attacked or harmed, either physically or emotionally

Some operators may be more familiar with the term 'at risk', however, in this book we use the term vulnerability.

Factors Making a Person Vulnerable

Age
Younger people tend to be more vulnerable to risk of harm. But age is not an overriding factor.
- Is the individual vulnerable due to their age, young or old?

Alone
When separated from friends, appearing lost or isolated, guest can be easily targeted.
- Where possible, attempts should be made to contact friends who may be able to assist.
- CCTV, ID scanners, etc. may well assist in identifying friends.
- Is there an opportunity to make contact with family?
- When refusing entry, make sure someone stays with the vulnerable person.

Overconsumption of Drugs & Alcohol
This will reduce inhibitions and decrease ability to make informed decisions. It changes perceptions of a person's own abilities and limitations, but the signs vary from being overly gregarious or passive, through to aggressive or a lack of spatial awareness. Sometimes guests appear unwell and usually experience a loss of motor skills.

If persons are ejected without their belongings, they may have no means

to contact anyone, no money and/or appropriate clothing, which may render the person vulnerable.
- How you can assist the person in getting home safely? Do you need to arrange a taxi?
- Is the individual/group so intoxicated that it is not reasonable to expect them to be able to take care of themselves?
- You have a responsibility to those refused entry, particularly if underage – do you have a child in front of you?
- Are they accompanied by others who may also be seeking entry – are they capable of taking responsibility for the individuals concerned?
- Seek assistance from a colleague where possible and obtain full details from emergency services, such as the call reference number.
- Ensure staff are aware of the location of the medical kit and ensure it is in date and the staff are trained to use it.

State of mind
The emotional or mental state that the guest is in can be influenced by a range of factors – friends will usually notice a difference in behaviours first.
- Staff must be aware of guests showing excessive emotions.
- Enlist a guest's friend to calm the person and help them get home safely.

Wearing Expensive Jewellery
A spate of watch thefts that occurred in London's West end and beyond has highlighted this issue. Many of the crimes occur after the guest has been followed home, thus making it difficult for the various local police forces to take effective action.
- Warn guests thieves operate in the area and to hide their valuables.
- Where possible, escort them to their taxis.
- Ensure staff outside are vigilant.

Presence of an Offender
Ultimately, the one thing that puts guests at risk from harm is usually the presence of an offender. Risk of potential harm increases substantially when the above factors are combined with the presence of a criminal offender.
- It's important to remember that anyone from any background can

commit an offence. Offenders can be predatory or opportunistic in nature. There is no one specific demographic relating to offenders.
- Offenders may be looking to target vulnerable people to commit crime or may be looking to take advantage of a situation for their own benefit.
- Almost 80% of sexual assaults are carried out by someone known to the victim.

Does the premises have an internal safe space? (WAVE Space)
Can you arrange a space that is considered the 'WAVE' space where the person can be supported until assistance can be arranged?
- A safe space could be a room or area where a vulnerable person can be taken and feel safe whilst arranging assistance.
- Facilities should be made available so that the vulnerable person can make contact with friends or family, receive medical assistance, or speak to an appropriate member of staff such as a welfare officer.
- If your premises does not have a safe (WAVE) space, are there any local safe havens?

Does the premises have a Welfare Officer? (WAVE Officer)
- It is important that the welfare officer is clearly identifiable to both customers and staff and has appropriate training, which should include vulnerability awareness and interventions training, conflict resolution, first aid, and crime response training.
- The Welfare Officer should have a current DBS (Disclosure and Barring Service) check.
- They may also be accredited by the Security Industry Authority (SIA) as a Door Supervisor (or Close Protection Officer).

Is there a Street Pastor available to assist?
- A street pastor is a volunteer who can provide support and care to vulnerable persons

Can we warn guest about potential offenders in the area?
- Cars driving around
- Watch thieves

How to Recognise Vulnerability

As always, early identification is key. Trust your instinct - if you have concerns then make an intervention. Use our SAAB (speech, attitude, appearance, and behaviour) methodology which we covered in the section on preventing intoxication to assess the guest. As a reminder, here are some highlights:

Recognising Vulnerability	
Unsteady on their feet	Drowsy
Incoherent	Upset
Irrational	Being controlled by somebody
Glazed eyes	Injury
Disheveled appearance	Quiet
Lost	Excitable
Alone	Missing clothing
Being plied with alcohol/drugs	Vomiting

Where can we intervene to reduce vulnerability?
- In the street
- In the premises
- Refusal of entry to premises
- Ejection from premises

Ask for Angela

Ask For Angela provides a useful additional tool for dealing with vulnerability.
- The 'Ask for Angela' initiative aims to reduce sexual violence and vulnerability by providing customers with a non-descript phrase they can use to gain assistance from staff members in order to be separated from the company of someone with whom they feel unsafe due to that person's actions, words or behaviour.
- By asking for Angela, an individual should be treated as a vulnerable person and the interventions you have in place should be applied.

STAYING OPEN

#ASK FOR ANGELA

> **Hi I'm Angela,**
>
> Are you on a date that isn't working out?
>
> Is your Tinder or POF date not who they said they were on their profile?
>
> Do you feel like you're not in a safe situation?
>
> Does it all feel a bit weird?
>
> If you go to the bar and ask for 'Angela' the bar staff will know you need some help getting out of your situation and will call you a taxi or help you out discreetly – without too much fuss

www.met.police.uk/AskforAngela

Call **101** for non-emergency enquiries, to report an incident or get help.

If you're deaf or hard of hearing, use our textphone service on **18001 101**.

Call **999** if it's an emergency or a crime is in progress.

METROPOLITAN POLICE

Safeguarding Departing Guests

Here is a sample policy to help safeguard departing guests:

1. Any information regarding thieves or suspicious activity in the vicinity of the premises will be reported to the police.

STAYING OPEN

2. *Any information or intelligence received from police will be included in pre-opening briefings with security and staff.*
3. *Signage will be displayed at the exit stating – "Thieves are operating in this area. If you are concerned for your safety, please speak to a member of staff".*
4. *Staff will receive Welfare and Vulnerability Engagement (WAVE) training.*
5. *Security and staff at the entrance will proactively monitor guests leaving. Any person who is considered to be at risk or vulnerable will be spoken to by a manager.*
6. *Any person considered vulnerable will engage the Guest Welfare Policy.*
7. *A taxi will be offered to any person who is considered to be at risk or vulnerable. If the person concerned has a car nearby, security will escort them to their vehicle. A note of the vehicle description and registration number will be recorded and retained.*
8. *Any intervention, or proactive action, will be recorded, including refused assistance.*
9. *Security will monitor the street and report any suspicious activity to the manager in charge.*
10. *Security equipped with Body Worn Cameras (BWC) will attempt to video any persons loitering or acting suspiciously in the immediate vicinity.*
11. *Any relevant information will be shared with neighbouring premises.*

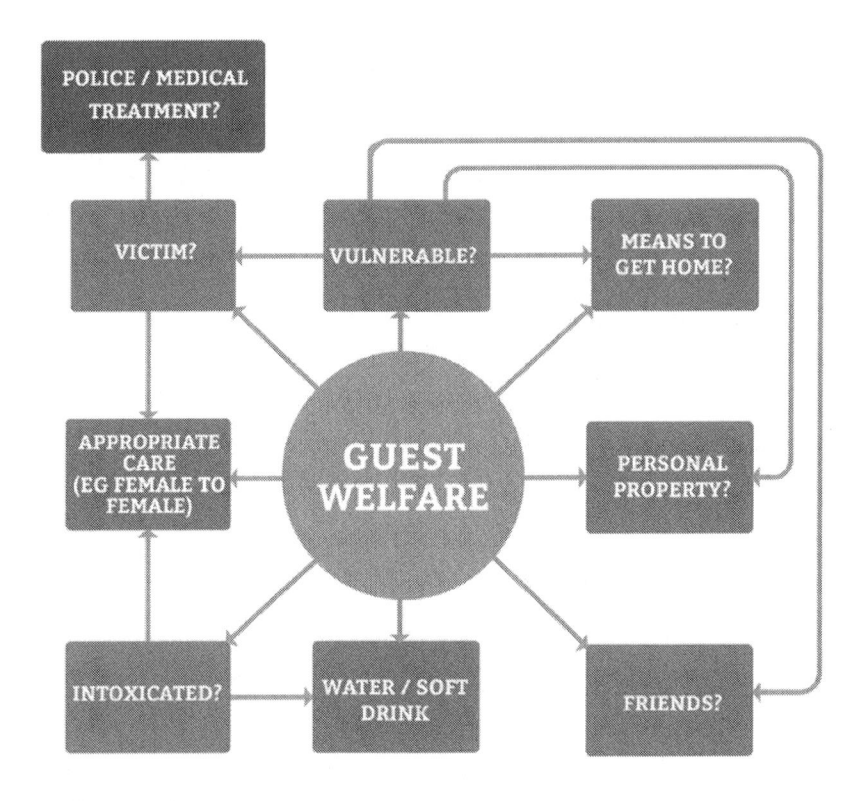

GUEST WELFARE

- POLICE / MEDICAL TREATMENT?
- VICTIM?
- VULNERABLE?
- MEANS TO GET HOME?
- APPROPRIATE CARE (EG FEMALE TO FEMALE)
- **GUEST WELFARE**
- PERSONAL PROPERTY?
- INTOXICATED?
- WATER / SOFT DRINK
- FRIENDS?

Victim Support
Provides help and information for anyone who has been affected by a crime, including a violent or physical assault, or is wary about involving the police. Helpline: 0845 30 30 900 (7 days a week) Website: www.victimsupport.org
The Rape and Sexual Abuse Support Centre
Support and information for women and girls who have been raped or sexually abused, however long ago and whatever the circumstance. Helpline: 0845 1221 331 (7 days a week) Website: www.rapecrisis.org.uk
NHS Direct
Provides confidential nurse advice and health information. The service can also help you find a local genitourinary medicine (GUM) clinic, where you can get checked for STIs. Helpline: 08457 4647 (7 days a week) Website: www.nhsdirect.org.uk
Terrence Higgins Trust
Practical support, help, counselling, and advice for anyone with, or concerned about, AIDS and HIV infection. Website: www.tht.org.uk
UK Police Service
Provides links to all official police forces across the country and related organisations. Call: 101 (999 in an emergency) Website: www.police.uk
Crimestoppers
The organisation works for you, your family, and your community to stop crime. You can call anonymously with information. Helpline: 0800 555 111 (7 days a week) Website: www.crimestoppers.org.uk

CHAPTER 16
Ejections

"Your demons may have been ejected from the building, but they're out in the parking lot, doing push-ups."

- Dan Harris

There are occasions when you will have to ask a guest to leave your premises. This normally falls into three categories:
1. For violent conduct (fighting or aggressive behaviour)
2. For non-violent conduct (being intoxicated)
3. Someone suspected of a crime that you will detain for the police

Your staff should be trained to identify when someone is intoxicated, causing trouble, or acting inappropriately. They always need to be vigilant and confident about taking action by calling a manager or security. For additional support, keep radios behind bars, in cloakrooms, and toilets as these can all be flashpoints where staff are often working alone.

Staff should be trained on how to use the radios, when to inform door supervisors and management of any concerns they have, and what to do if they have witnessed an incident. If they are approached by a guest in distress or if they need assistance, they must react immediately and call for help.

As far as possible, security should deal with any potentially violent situation, NOT bar staff. In all instances, the situation must be dealt with calmly and professionally. Staff should follow a strict procedure which is set out to ensure safe ejection for both the customer, door supervisors, and employees whilst causing minimum disruption to other guests.

For minor misdemeanours (for example, refusing to move away from a designated fire exit or standing on a chair), consider issuing a first warning. If there is a further instance of misbehaviour, the persons should be ejected using a hands-off policy. At any time, a Customer Code of Conduct may be quoted.

Process of Ejection

The following is a summary of the process that should apply if an ejection is required. Please note that you need to consider the peculiarities of your venue and staffing situation and develop your own process that is most effective:

1. **Ensure you understand the situation and assess it first**

Always take account of the whole situation, for example, those involved may be with a large group of friends who may react violently.

2. **Ensure you have support**

Before taking any form of action, call a manager and security for assistance.

3. **Explain the reasons why a person is being ejected**

It is often better to inform their friends first of what is about to happen so they don't react badly. Remember, if you embarrass someone or cause them to lose face, the situation may quickly escalate.

The reasons for being asked to leave need to be clear; you may find it is easier to ask someone to get some fresh air for 10 minutes.

4. **All guests should voluntarily walk out**

This is often called a 'hands off ejection'. Wherever possible, persons being ejected should not be touched, although by law, reasonable force may be used. You always need to be careful when using any force if you think it is 'reasonable'.

5. **Use the front entrance where possible and use your radio to inform the door**

If there is a confrontation between guests that you fear could escalate or there is a situation that disrupts the business, both parties should be ejected. In this situation, use more than one exit or delay one party leaving to avoid further confrontation outside.

The senior manager on duty or the Designated Premises Supervisor should have the final say on who is ejected following any confrontation in the premises.

In all cases, a record should be kept of all ejections. Where any force has been used, a full incident report should be written. If the authorities require further statements and/or your attendance is required at a police station, this should be done immediately or at the police's request.

Always remember you are trying to de-escalate a situation; be discreet and try to avoid embarrassment. Be confident in your delivery but don't raise your voice. Clearly explain the reason for why they are being asked to leave or get some fresh air.

Below are some suggested scripts that can be used but each situation will be different so use your experience and best judgement:
- If speaking to their friends first: *"Look, I can see you are all having a good time. Unfortunately, your friend there is acting inappropriately or is intoxicated, and we need to take them outside for some fresh air and water. We want you all to continue enjoying your night, but we need one of you to come with your friend to help look after them."*
- Or to the person directly: *"We want you to have a good time, but we need you to come outside for some fresh air and water for a few minutes – please can you come with us. One of your friends is going to come with you."*

Should the customer not understand the reason after two explanations or they refuse to cooperate, disengage and hand responsibility to security who will advise the customer that they will be shown the route off-site. The manager should always observe their removal.

Should a physical ejection be necessary, only reasonable force will be used. There is more detail on this subject further on, but any force should be a last resort.
- Offer to find the friends if they are not already with them and collect any coat or personal belongings they have left in the venue. Always remember GUEST WELFARE. The customer will remain with the manager and the member of security while these happen.
- Give advice on how to get home safely.
- Get their friends to look after them or, if appropriate, pay for a taxi home.

- If a customer is being collected and it is safe to allow them to wait to be picked up, an appropriate area should be available for them with security presence.
- The customer should be offered a bottle of water in the meantime.
- Take the details and description of any customer being ejected from the venue and make a written record.

The Use of Reasonable Force

Remember that you will always have to able to explain and justify your actions, perhaps even in legal proceedings, so think before acting and remember your conflict management training.

These questions are not a definitive list but will give you a sense of what you need to assess a physical ejection.
- Is it absolutely NECESSARY to use force?
- What amount of force is REASONABLE to eject the person?
- Consider the size and build of the person to be ejected
- Are any weapons used or a threat from the person to be ejected?
- When is force no longer required?

For further clarity, let's look at the words NECESSARY and REASONABLE in more detail.

NECESSARY

The law is quite clear on the term 'necessary' with regards to the use of force. Necessary force is not what is deemed necessary by someone considering the facts from a safe and comfortable place well after the events, but what the person carrying out the acts in question considered necessary at the time. Only you can say why you thought it necessary to use the force at the time, whereas a court may have to ultimately decide whether the amount of force used was reasonable or not.

REASONABLE

The term 'reasonable' is more difficult to define and not always easy. It will depend on the circumstances and careful thought will need to be given when you assess the seriousness of the threat.

Ask yourself the question!

Would it be reasonable to punch or use physical force on someone who is verbally abusing you? The answer is no.

Physical force should only be considered when there is a real possibility of physical harm to you or someone else and even then, the amount of force used should be appropriate and reasonable to the situation.

A door supervisor or manager claiming self-defence as an excuse for the use of force must be able to show that:
1. They did not want to fight
2. They responded with no more force than was reasonable to repel the attack

If you can demonstrate those two things, force is not unlawful and no criminal offence is committed.

If, however, the force continues outside (having used reasonable force inside) to 'teach them a lesson' or to 'stop them coming back again', then that extra and unnecessary use of force would not be seen as 'reasonable' and would make you or the door supervisor liable to criminal proceedings for assault.

Remember
The test of whether force is reasonable in any given circumstance is a subjective one and is assessed on the facts as the person concerned believed them to be at the time. As such, a full incident report should be written whenever force is used to eject a customer.

Ejection Required

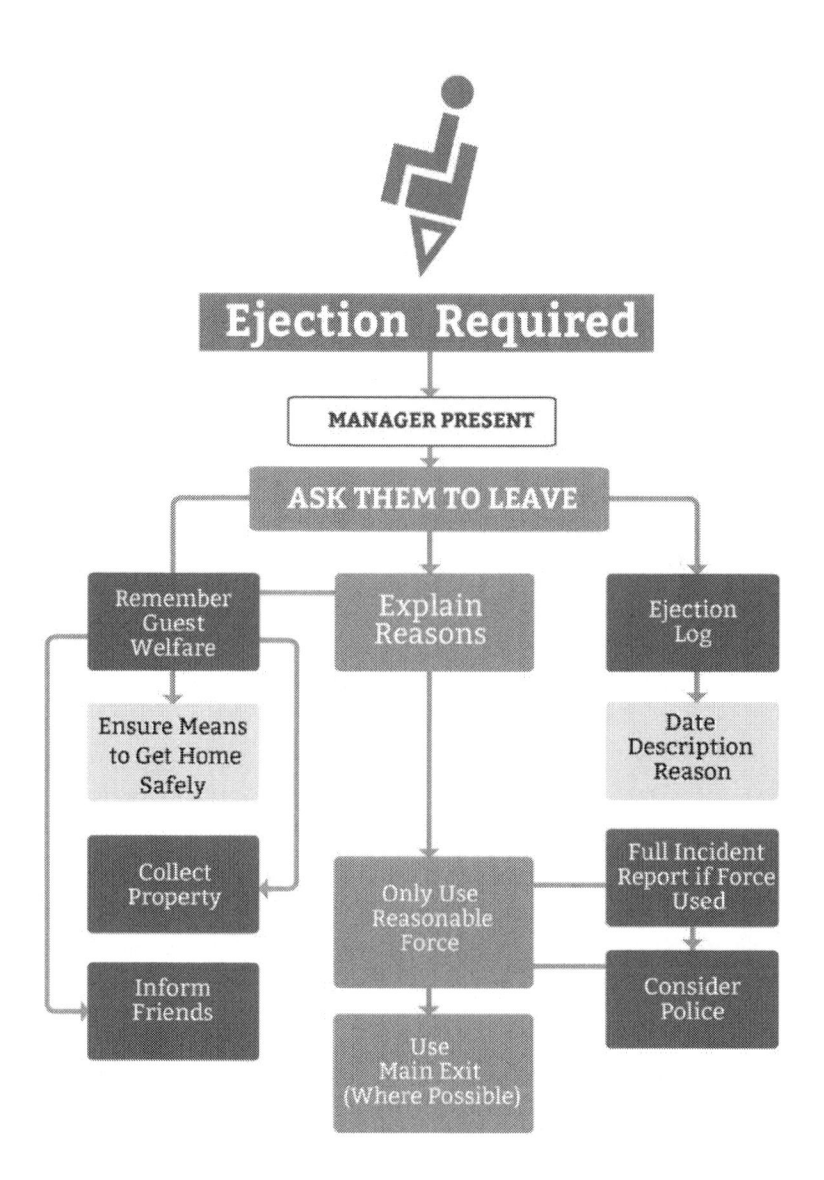

MANAGER PRESENT

ASK THEM TO LEAVE

- Remember Guest Welfare
  - Ensure Means to Get Home Safely
  - Collect Property
  - Inform Friends
- Explain Reasons
  - Only Use Reasonable Force
  - Use Main Exit (Where Possible)
- Ejection Log
  - Date Description Reason
  - Full Incident Report if Force Used
  - Consider Police

STAYING OPEN

1. THE SIGNS → 2. GET IN THE ZONE → 3. RESOLVING → 4. POST INCIDENT

1. THE SIGNS

Fight or Flight
Instinctive Response to Threat Prepares Body for Action

Triggers
Embarassment
Patronised
Loss of Face
Ignored
Rudeness
Ridiculed
Not Taken Seriously

Inhibitors
Social/Legal Consequences
Self Control
Personal Values
Fear Opponent May Fight Back

Escalation
Intense Eye Contact
Personal Abuse
Increasingly Vulgar
Threatening Language
Invading Personal Space
Pointing
Physical Contact
Squaring Up
Posture

2. GET IN THE ZONE

S.A.F.E.R.
S - Step Back
A - Assess Threat
F - Find Help
E - Evaluate Options
R - Respond

P.O.P.S.
P - Person
O - Object
P - Place
S - Situation

Communication
Words: 7%
Tone: 38%
Non Verbal: 55%
Noise
Drink / Drugs
Language Emotion
Culture
Ego Mental Health
Authority

Remember
Manage the Gap
Customer Expectations Be Professional
Be Friendly & Approachable but not an 'Easy Touch'

3. RESOLVING

Signal Non Agression
P.A.L.M.S.
P - Position
A - Attitude
L - Look & Listen
M - Make Space
S - Stance & Space

Open Palms
Empathy
Actively Listening

Remember
Alert Other Staff Try to Build Rapport
Switch If You Need To Try To Diffuse (with Offer / Gift)
Don't Get Angry
Manage Abuse
Maintain Positive Attitude
Be Assertive

Drawing a Line
May Lead to Escalation
Try to Choose Time/ Place

Escorting Drills
Be Alert

4. POST INCIDENT

What To Do Next?
Incident Report
Post Incident Analysis
Support for Staff

Learn From Incident
What Happened?
What Could Have Been Done Differently?
Good Practices
Ensure Lessons Are Learnt
How Others Can be Informed

My Attitude — Affects — Your Behaviour
Your Behaviour — Affects — My Attitude
My Behaviour — Affects — Your Attitude
Your Attitude — Affects — My Behaviour

CHAPTER 17
Dealing with Serious Incidents

"If you can meet with Triumph and Disaster, and treat those two impostors just the same"
- Rudyard Kipling

One of the manager's key responsibilities is to deal with a serious incident properly and effectively. In our experience as consultants, we often find that premises are judged more on post-incident actions than the incident itself.

In this chapter, we consider the various measures to take following a serious incident and why they are a necessity.

For the purposes of this chapter, we will define a serious incident as the following:
- An injury due to some form of weapon (e.g., knife, bottle, pole, etc.)
- An assault that caused a broken skin injury
- An incident which resulted in death or serious injury. (i.e., heart failure, accident, serious assault, etc.)
- Any other crime committed where police may need to search and investigate for any evidence

In the event of a serious incident, the manager in charge should call the police or appropriate emergency service immediately and confirm that the police have been informed (and any other appropriate emergency service). You should ask for a CAD number which is a unique reference for that day.

The senior manager should always meet and brief the first police officer on scene to ensure clear communication and appropriate actions are carried out upon police instructions.

Ensure that adequate victim welfare and any medical assistance required is provided and, if safe to do so, locate and detain offender(s). Suspects should be held away from any victim by security pending arrival of police.

Identify and secure any crime scene(s). Evacuate the area where the incident occurred and preserve the scene – do not move any objects, furniture, bottles, glasses etc. (see the Crime Scene Preservation chapter for more information).

Identify any witnesses and keep them on the premises for police or, if this is not possible, obtain contact details.

Retrieve any relevant CCTV and supply all images required to police. If possible, transfer them to separate media to give to police attending the incident.

Ensure all staff involved write comprehensive accounts of the incident and, if requested, give statements to police. All staff should remain on the premises until no longer required by police.

Investigate: Who? What? When? Where?

As the manager of the premises, you need to quickly ascertain the nature of the incident. Do NOT make assumptions – find out the facts by speaking to witnesses (customers and staff), especially any person who may have an injury.

- WHAT do you see? – broken glass, wet floor, blood?
- WHERE do you see it? – in which areas of the venue?
- WHEN did it happen? – treat and speak to injured person(s)
- WHO was involved? – trace the offender (if there is one) and view CCTV

You will need to write a full incident report. This may take the form of a composite report that includes various accounts from your staff, and may then need to be updated in the following days as you receive further information or there are events related to the incident (e.g. police collecting CCTV, a witness coming forward, etc.). You may also want to add additional content to the report such as remedial action taken (e.g.

staff training).

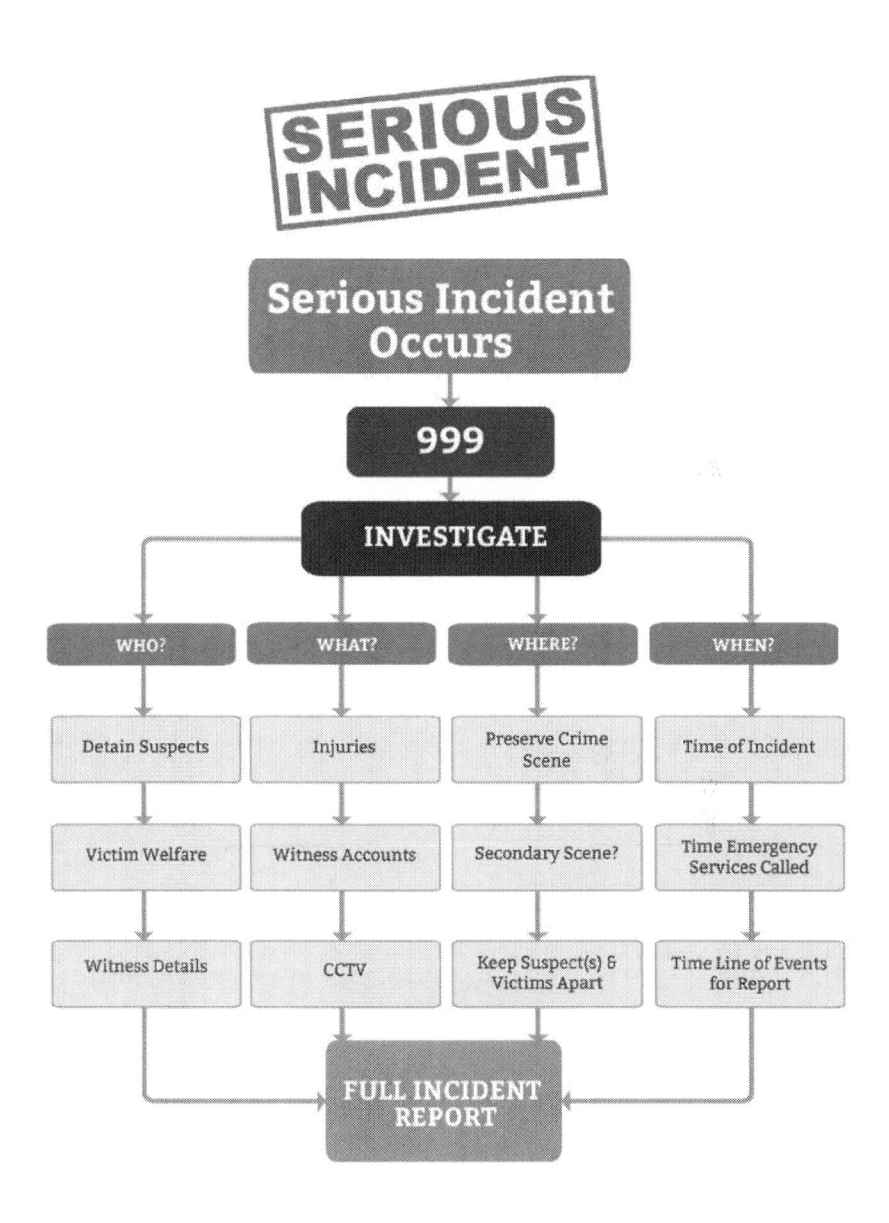

SERIOUS INCIDENT

Serious Incident Occurs

↓

999

↓

INVESTIGATE

WHO?	WHAT?	WHERE?	WHEN?
Detain Suspects	Injuries	Preserve Crime Scene	Time of Incident
Victim Welfare	Witness Accounts	Secondary Scene?	Time Emergency Services Called
Witness Details	CCTV	Keep Suspect(s) & Victims Apart	Time Line of Events for Report

↓

FULL INCIDENT REPORT

CHAPTER 18
Crime Scene Preservation

"Any action of an individual, and obviously, the violent action constituting a crime, cannot occur without leaving a trace."
- Dr Edmond Locard [Translated]

When there has been a serious incident and police need to search and investigate for any evidence, the crime scene must be preserved as much as possible.

Useful definitions

- Crime Scene: Any physical location in which a crime has occurred or is suspected of having occurred
- Primary Scene: The original location
- Secondary Scene: An alternate location where additional evidence may be found
- Physical Evidence: Any material items present at the crime scene, on victims, or found in the suspect's possession
- Suspect: Person thought to have committed a crime
- Accomplice: Person associated with the suspect
- Testimonial Evidence: Oral or written statements given to police or in court

Valuable evidence can be lost within seconds following an incident, making the police's job much more difficult to trace and prosecute any offenders. To ensure the preservation of any vital forensic evidence, management needs to immediately take charge of any scene following a serious incident.

There are four important principles to good scene preservation:

1. Preventing evidence from being contaminated (i.e. leaving a glass at the scene which was not there at the time of the incident)
2. Preventing evidence from being destroyed (i.e. by someone walking through the area and treading on evidence)
3. Preventing evidence from being removed (i.e. glasses or weapons being moved or furniture being re-arranged)
4. Preventing evidence from being moved (i.e. unnecessary tidying up when the positions of items may be of importance)

The responsibility to preserve a potential crime scene and for all events following an incident should be taken by the senior manager on duty. This includes preserving the scene, incident reporting, downloading the CCTV and body cam footage, and liaising with police on the night. Any co-operative witnesses are to be taken to a holding area and the senior manager is to inform the first attending officer.

Once an area has been declared as a crime scene by the senior manager on duty, then all access to the area must cease immediately. Generally, crime scenes are preserved by marked off areas with by barriers, ropes, chairs, or tables as well as security.

Any evidence must be left where it falls (broken glass, bottles, etc.) unless it is dangerous to leave it where it is. If it must be moved, a manager must pick it up using gloves (avoiding fingerprints) and place it inside a police evidence bag if possible. It should then be signed and sealed and placed in the safe to hand over to police on their request. Secondary scenes need to be protected and treated the same.

Individuals may also be considered crime scenes and all precaution must be taken to prevent the transfer of evidence. For example, a door supervisor who has restrained a suspect for assault should not then have contact with a victim. A suspect and victim should also be kept apart.

A manager on duty should remain at the crime scene until the police arrive.

A preserved crime scene must always take precedent over the financial needs of the business. Whenever possible, if a crime scene can be preserved without disruption to the general public, then the premises should run as normal. If the crime scene disrupts the use of one of the fire exits, then the front door should be closed to the public immediately and a view will be taken as to whether trading will continue. If the crime scene will either greatly disrupt the public or jeopardise public safety, then the senior manager on duty will be responsible for the decision to close.

Witnesses to the incident are to be asked to remain inside the premises and, if possible, they are to be seated in an area away from other customers. Free, non-alcoholic refreshments (such as coffee or water) should be offered to them to assist in their comfort.

Above all, victim care must be considered when dealing with vulnerable people.

Remember

- Protect the crime scene to preserve its physical aspects.
- Steps need to be taken as soon possible after the incident, even while victims are being attended to.
- Cordon off if possible or station staff in relevant positions to reroute traffic.
- Prevent unnecessary walking around and intrusions.
- Prevent unneeded movement or touching of physical evidence.
- Do not allow any items to be removed from the scene without permission from authorities.
- Do not discuss the crime with witnesses or bystanders.
- Be alert to secondary scenes – for example, a weapon discarded in toilets or exits.
- Follow the same procedures for the secondary scene as the primary scene.
- People can also be crime scenes, so avoid transfer of evidence.

STAYING OPEN

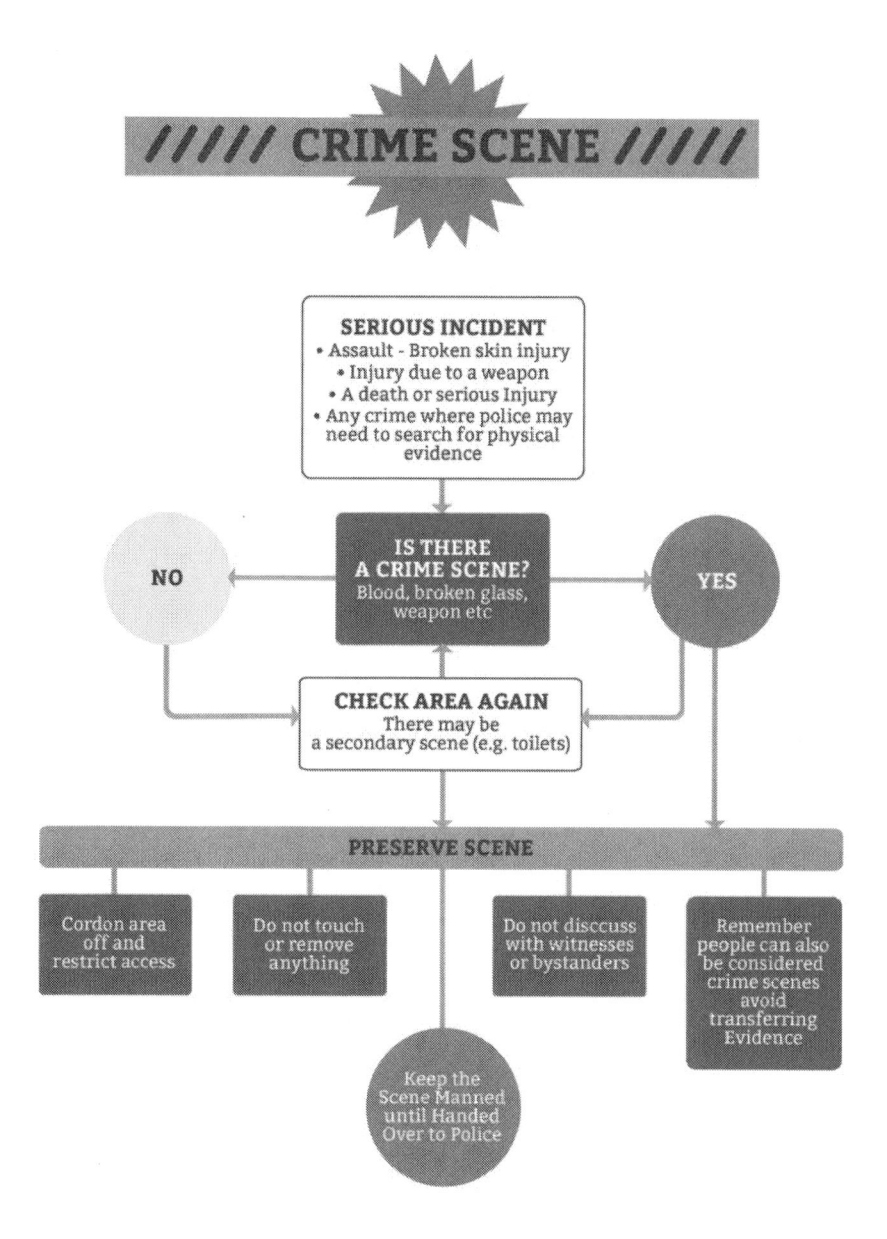

CRIME SCENE

SERIOUS INCIDENT
- Assault - Broken skin injury
- Injury due to a weapon
- A death or serious Injury
- Any crime where police may need to search for physical evidence

IS THERE A CRIME SCENE?
Blood, broken glass, weapon etc

- NO
- YES

CHECK AREA AGAIN
There may be a secondary scene (e.g. toilets)

PRESERVE SCENE

- Cordon area off and restrict access
- Do not touch or remove anything
- Do not disccuss with witnesses or bystanders
- Remember people can also be considered crime scenes avoid transferring Evidence

Keep the Scene Manned until Handed Over to Police

CHAPTER 19
Incident Reporting and Investigating

"It has long been an axiom of mine that the little things are infinitely the most important. "

- Arthur Conan Doyle

The aim of this chapter is to inform you of the actions you need to take following an incident and to give you the skills required to accurately record accident/incident investigations.

Incidents vs Accidents

Incident
This can refer to any event – big or small, good or bad, intentional or unintentional. For example:
- A disagreement among patrons
- An ejection
- Someone falling over but not hurting themselves
- Near misses

Accident
This is an unwanted, unplanned event that leads to loss or injury.

An example of a minor accident is when you step on someone's foot or spill your coffee on them. However, stepping on someone's foot causing them to fall downstairs and break a leg is an example of a major accident. In both cases, you did not want or plan to do it.

In terms of licensing, the traditional definition of an incident becomes blurred. Security ejecting someone causing an injury unintentionally, technically, is an accident. But we would normally talk of it as an incident. Police talk about incidents involving staff, not accidents.

For the sake of continuity and common practice, we will continue to refer to these events as incidents.

All incidents should be investigated and reported, and the level of investigation should be based on the potential worst consequence of the accident or incident.

In almost all cases, 'non-injury' incidents will have had the potential to become events with more serious consequences. Incidents always have an immediate and underlying cause and root cause.

Recording of Incidents

Accurate details of any incident must be recorded at the time in case there is an investigation at a later date and to show that any incident was dealt with correctly.

The following incidents should all be fully reported:
- All crimes reported to the venue
- All ejections of patrons where there has been physical force used
- Any complaints received relating to the four licensing objectives
- Any incidents of disorder or violence
- Seizures of drugs or offensive weapons
- Any faults in the CCTV system
- Any visit by a relevant authority or emergency service
- Any emergency situation such a fire, flood, loss of power, or bomb threat
- Any accident or injury to employee, contractor, or customer

Each incident report should contain the following:
- The full name and position of the person reporting
- Their SIA registration if security
- Date, time, and location of incident
- Whether the incident was captured by CCTV and which camera – have the images been burnt onto DVD?
- Was a crime scene preserved?
- Full details of the incident
- Whether the police were called (and who called them)
- Police CAD number (if police were called)

- Whether police attended (if so, provide shoulder numbers)
- Whether anyone was injured (give full details, including any medical assistance given and whether an ambulance attended)
- Describe all persons involved in the incident
- Give details of all witnesses to the incident

DO NOT:
- Use slang
- Use acronyms, abbreviations or terminology that may not be understood
- Make assumptions or speculate – be factual

Incident Response: What to Do in the Event of an Incident

There are generally three steps to take in the event of an incident:
1. Emergency Response
2. Initial Response and Assessment – carry out investigation
3. Incident Report

Emergency Response – take prompt emergency action
- Make the area safe
- Administer First Aid
- Call an ambulance and police if you need to

Initial Response and Assessment – carry out investigation (as soon as possible)
- Preserve the crime scene
- Photograph the scene – take a lot of photos
- Get the names of witnesses and anyone present
- Note who was involved, where they were, and relevant positions of witnesses
- Note the condition of the area (orderliness, tidiness, wet surface, obstacles, hazards, etc.)
- Download CCTV

Report the event to the senior manager who will decide on what action should be taken if not already done so.

Incident Report – investigation guide
An incident report needs to include all the essential information about the incident or near-miss. The report-writing process begins with fact-finding and ends with recommendations for preventing future accidents.

There are four basic steps:
- A. Find the Facts
- B. Determine the Sequence
- C. Analyse
- D. Recommend

A. Find the Facts

To prepare for writing an accident report, you have to gather and record all the facts. For example:
- Date, time, and specific location of incident
- Names, job titles, and department of employees involved and immediate supervisor(s)
- Names and accounts of witnesses
- Events leading up to incident
- Exactly what the employee/guest was doing at the moment of the incident
- Environmental conditions (e.g. slippery floor, inadequate lighting, noise, etc.)
- Circumstances (including tasks, equipment, tools, materials, PPE, etc.)
- Specific injuries (including part(s) of body injured and nature and extent of injuries)
- Type of treatment for injuries
- Damage to equipment, materials, etc.

As a guide, when interviewing witnesses:
- Do so as soon as possible after the event
- Interview in familiar surroundings to avoid making the person unnecessarily uncomfortable
- Keep witnesses apart so they do not influence each other
- Avoid blaming anyone – do not lead the witness
- **If you have the helpful BETTER Compliance Incident Reporting Tool, use that to fill in the details**

B. Determine the Sequence

Based on the facts and using CCTV, you should be able to determine the sequence of events. In your report, describe this sequence in detail, including:
- Events leading up to the incident – was the employee/guest arguing, acting abnormally, dancing wildly, making unwanted

advances, drinking heavily, falling over, etc.?
- Events involved in the incident – was the victim struck by an object or caught in/on/between objects? Where their third parties involved?
- Events immediately following the incident – what did the employee/guest do? Put a hand over a bleeding wound? Retaliate? Also, describe how other staff and guests responded. Did they call for help, administer first aid, shut down the area, move the victim, etc.?

The incident should be described in the report in sufficient detail that any reader can clearly picture what happened. You might consider creating a diagram to show, in a simple and visually effective manner, the sequence of events related to the incident and include this in your incident report. You might also wish to include photos of the incident scene, which may help readers follow the sequence of events.

C. Analyse
- 'Immediate' causes tend to be unsafe acts or conditions.
- 'Underlying' causes tend to be the reasons for the unsafe acts or conditions.
- 'Root' causes tend to be failures in management control and/or the safety management system.

For example, someone starts a fight with another guest in the queue. The immediate cause is the aggressive guest starting to swing punches. The underlying cause is that some guests are jumping the queue. The root cause is that the queue was not being managed correctly with a proper system in place.

D. Recommend
Recommendations for corrective action might include immediate corrective action as well as long-term corrective actions such as:
- Employee training on preventative techniques
- Preventative maintenance activities on CCTV that is not working or relocation of cameras to newly discovered black spots
- Evaluation of job procedures with a recommendation for changes
- Conducting a job hazard analysis to evaluate the risk to employees and guest going forward
- Engineering changes that make the area safer – improving lighting or moving furniture to improve the flow of people

Also Remember:
- The Accident Book needs to be filled in (even for minor accidents)
- RIDDO (Reporting of Injuries, Diseases & Dangerous Occurrences)
- To notify insurers

RIDDO (Reporting of Injuries, Diseases & Dangerous Occurrences)

Certain accidents are RIDDO reportable. If someone has died or has been injured because of a work-related accident, this may have to be reported to the Health & Safety Executive. The accident that caused the death or injury must be connected to the work activity.

Types of reportable injury
- Deaths
- Major injuries
- Over-three-day injuries
- People not at work
- Where a member of the public or person who is not at work has died
- Injuries to members of the public or people not at work where they are taken from the scene of an accident to hospital for treatment.

In addition, if there has been an accident a report must be completed in the Accident Report Book. Please see your Health and Safety Policy for further information on reporting accidents.

Taking Witness Statements

When writing a witness statement, make sure it contains the following information:
1. Provide your full name, age (e.g. over 18), and occupation
2. Give details of any professional qualifications (e.g. Personal Licence, SIA registration)
3. Start with how long you have worked at the premises and your general responsibilities
4. Next begin your record of the incident (the day, date, time, and place)

5. Only write facts you know to be true (i.e. what you have seen and heard)
6. Be clear and coherent – do not ramble
7. Use your timeline – keep events in chronological order
8. Use first person singular, "I spoke to Mr Smith" rather than "Mr Smith was spoken to" to minimise ambiguity
9. Avoid abbreviations and technical terms that are not generally known
10. If you are not certain about your recollections, make this clear. It is important that the statement is accurate
11. Always sign and date your statement
12. Before signing, always read your statement to ensure it is correct
13. Keep a copy of your statement

STAYING OPEN

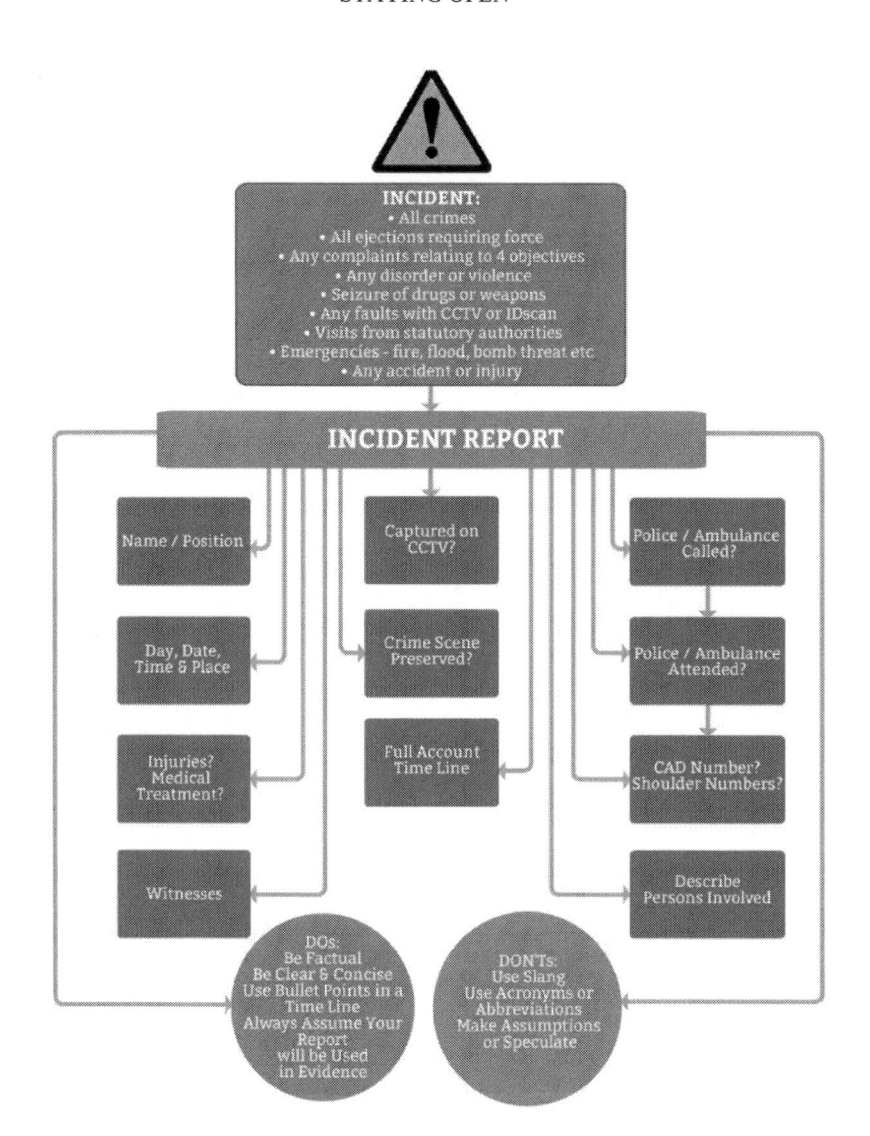

INCIDENT:
- All crimes
- All ejections requiring force
- Any complaints relating to 4 objectives
- Any disorder or violence
- Seizure of drugs or weapons
- Any faults with CCTV or IDscan
- Visits from statutory authorities
- Emergencies - fire, flood, bomb threat etc
- Any accident or injury

INCIDENT REPORT

- Name / Position
- Day, Date, Time & Place
- Injuries? Medical Treatment?
- Witnesses
- Captured on CCTV?
- Crime Scene Preserved?
- Full Account Time Line
- Police / Ambulance Called?
- Police / Ambulance Attended?
- CAD Number? Shoulder Numbers?
- Describe Persons Involved

DOs:
Be Factual
Be Clear & Concise
Use Bullet Points in a Time Line
Always Assume Your Report will be Used in Evidence

DON'Ts:
Use Slang
Use Acronyms or Abbreviations
Make Assumptions or Speculate

SECTION 4
Consequences

CHAPTER 20
Remedial Action and Closure Powers

"In nature there are neither rewards nor punishments; there are consequences."
- Robert Green Ingersoll

The authorities have a wide array of powers to deal with problem premises. Managers must fully understand the closure powers available to the statutory authorities and the possible consequences of remedial action.

Review of Premises Licence S.51 Licensing Act 2003

Any interested party or a responsible authority can ask the licensing authority to review a premises licences because of a matter arising in connection with one or more of the four licensing objectives.

A review will only be 'relevant' if it relates to the adverse effect of the licensed premises on the promotion of at least one of the licensing objectives. This means that the request for review will need to demonstrate that the operation of the premises licence undermines one of the four licensing objectives.

Upon receipt of a valid application for review the licensing authority will:
- Advertise the review for 28 days, from the day after the application was made:
    - at, or near the site of the premises to which the application relates (and where it can conveniently be read from the exterior)
    - at the Licensing Authority (normally on an on-line licensing

register)

During the 28-day consultation period, a responsible authority or any other person may submit representations to the licensing authority in connection with the review.

The licensing authority will consider the review application and any relevant representations that have been made at a licensing panel hearing. This will be held within 28 days of the end of the 28-day consultation period.

The options open to the licensing authority at the hearing include:
- Modify the conditions of the premises licence, for example, by reducing the hours of opening or by requiring door supervisors at particular times.
- Exclude a licensable activity from the scope of the licence.
- Remove the designated premises supervisor, for example, because they consider that the problems are the result of poor management.
- Suspend the licence for a period not exceeding three months.
- Revoke the licence.

Example
A resident is regularly disturbed by loud music and rowdy customers of a pub close to their home. They apply for a review of the pub's premises licence on the grounds that the public nuisance objective is not being promoted. At the hearing, the licensing committee decides to add licence conditions requiring the pub to install a noise limiter and implement a dispersal policy.

Summary Review S.53A Licensing Act 2003
The police may apply to the licensing authority for an expedited review of a premises licence where there is serious crime or serious disorder (or both). The licensing authority must, within 48 hours, consider whether it is necessary to take interim steps pending a full review hearing.

The options open to the licensing authority at the interim steps stage include:
- Modification of the conditions of the premises licence.
- The exclusion of the sale of alcohol by retail from the scope of the licence.

- Removal of the designated premises supervisor from the licence.
- Suspension of the licence.

After 28 days, a full review hearing is held and the licensing authority may take any of the previous steps or, in extreme cases, revoke the premises licence.

Example

Police apply for a summary review of a night club where there has been a gang-related stabbing. They believe there is a high risk of further serious violence at the premises. At the interim hearing, the committee suspends the licence pending a full hearing. The committee adds licence conditions in relation to searching and additional door supervisors.

It is very important to understand that any interim steps may apply if the decision at the second committee (full) hearing is appealed. For example, if your licence is suspended as an interim step and at the full hearing your licence is revoked, on appeal the suspension will apply until the matter is decided at the appeal hearing. This is a consequence of an important legal case R (o.a.o. 93 Feet East Ltd) v Tower Hamlets LBC (16th July 2013).

Other courses of action available to the authorities include:
- Section 19 Criminal Justice and Police Act 2001 (Closure Notice)
- Section 169A Licensing Act 2003 Closure notice for persistently selling alcohol to children
- S160 Licensing Act 2003 Order to close premises in an area experiencing disorder

It is very important that you seek legal advice if you are threatened with enforcement action

CLOSURE POWERS

'Closure' for Unauthorised Sales of Alcohol (Can Include Sales Not In Accordance with Authorisation of Licence e.g. in Breach of Conditions) S.19 Criminal Justice and Police Act 2001
By: Police Consequence: Possible Closure Under S.20 Until Such Time as Police / Licensing Authority See Need for Closure has Ceased

Voluntary Closure
By: You or at Police Request
Consequence: Could Possibly Avoid Forced Closure, Can Re-Open at Any Time, Gives You Time to Address Any Issues

Summary Review of Premises Licence S.53A Licensing Act 2003
By: Police
Consequence: Hearing within 48 Hours, Possible Interim Steps (incl. Suspension of Licence, Modified Conditions / Hours etc), Full Review Hearing Within 28 Days

CRIME & DISORDER

Closure Notice for Persistently Selling Alcohol to Children S.169A Licensing Act 2003
By: Police or Trading Standards
Consequence: Closure Not Exceeding 48 Hours

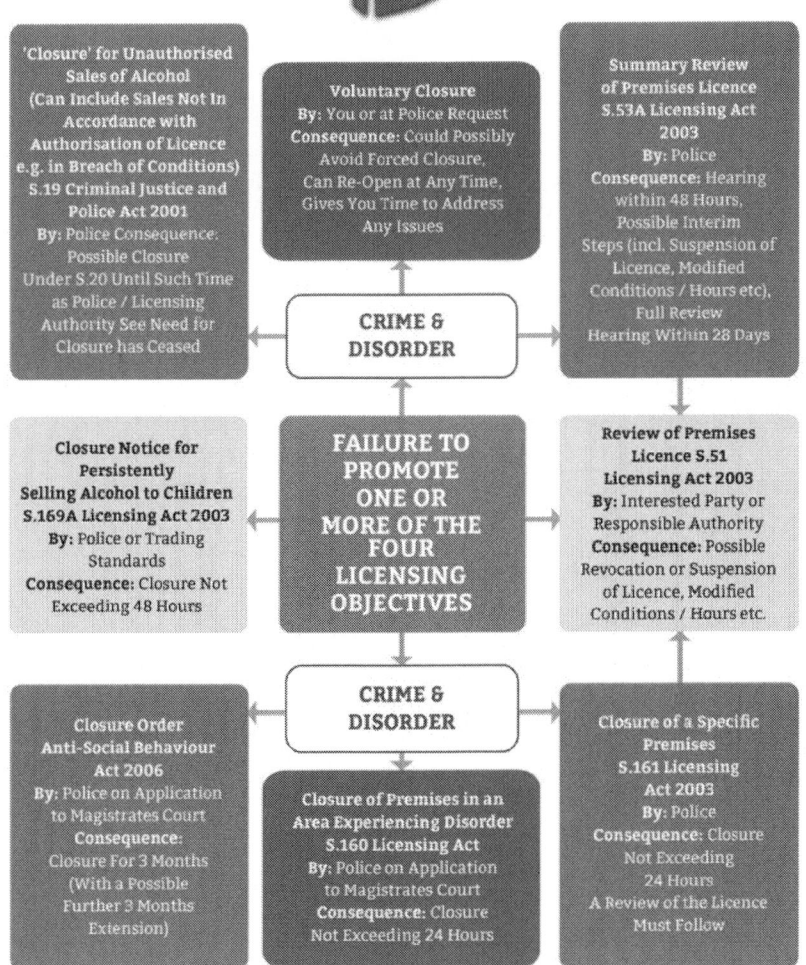

FAILURE TO PROMOTE ONE OR MORE OF THE FOUR LICENSING OBJECTIVES

Review of Premises Licence S.51 Licensing Act 2003
By: Interested Party or Responsible Authority
Consequence: Possible Revocation or Suspension of Licence, Modified Conditions / Hours etc.

CRIME & DISORDER

Closure Order Anti-Social Behaviour Act 2006
By: Police on Application to Magistrates Court
Consequence: Closure For 3 Months (With a Possible Further 3 Months Extension)

Closure of Premises in an Area Experiencing Disorder S.160 Licensing Act
By: Police on Application to Magistrates Court
Consequence: Closure Not Exceeding 24 Hours

Closure of a Specific Premises S.161 Licensing Act 2003
By: Police
Consequence: Closure Not Exceeding 24 Hours A Review of the Licence Must Follow

SECTION 5
Dealing with The Statutory Authorities

CHAPTER 21
Successfully Dealing with Inspections

"The trouble with most of us is that we'd rather be ruined by praise than saved by criticism."
- Norman Vincent Peale

Dealing with external regulatory bodies, enforcement agencies, and statutory inspections is an art form. But the visit of any enforcement officer need not be a stressful event. Any interaction with the authorities should be seen as an opportunity to impress.

Nature of the Problem

After all the hard work you and your staff have put into the area of compliance – the ongoing training, the due diligence records, and the policies and procedures – it often comes down to a particular inspector turning up on a particular day to take a snapshot of your business, dealing with whatever staff members happen to be on duty at the time.

No doubt you would assume that everyone in the industry, particularly your own business, would be accommodating, helpful, and polite in their dealings with the authorities. However, this is often not the case.

Whether it is the pressure, defensiveness, the fear of doing or saying the wrong thing, the uncertainty of what to do, lack of knowledge, or just complete lack of professionalism, many inspections go badly wrong purely because of the bad attitude and negative reaction of the manager and staff who happen to be on duty at the time.

Many owners and senior managers are mortified when visit reports are read back to them about how an inspector was kept waiting at the door for 30 minutes or told to come back at another time or was just rudely treated on the whole.

There is something about dealing with the statutory authorities that, for various reasons, seems to bring out the worst in many staff. But this need not be the case.

Remember, the whole tone and approach of an enforcement officer's inspection can be dictated within a few minutes of arriving at your premises – first impressions count!

Confidence and Competency

Having analysed many successful and unsuccessful inspections, we've learned it comes down to two things – confidence and competency, which come from the following:
- Knowing what is expected during the inspection
- Understanding the law and licence conditions relating to your premises
- Knowing how to behave during the visit
- Knowing where your paperwork is located
- Knowing what is in that paperwork and what it means
- Paperwork that it is up to date and complete
- Paperwork that is sufficient and compliant
- Having systems and training regimes in place
- Having a well-managed and maintained premises

The authorities are not there to trip you up; they don't want to have to go away and write voluminous reports if they don't have to. If you have the right attitude, they actually want you to succeed.

This is the opportunity for the business to shine and put you in a positive light. It should also help you establish a better working relationship with authorities.

Inspectors from enforcement agencies have certain statutory powers which include the right to enter premises for the purposes of inspection and other matters. Although they may be able to enter premises without notice, some may contact you in advance to arrange a formal inspection/visit.

Top Inspection Tips

- We repeat, the whole tone and approach of an enforcement officer's inspection can be dictated within a few minutes of arriving at your premises – first impressions count! Your security are often the first people the statutory authorities meet so it is crucial they know how to behave and what to say.
- Be confident, friendly and knowledgeable – but also listen to what an officer has to say.
- Ensure there are staff on duty who are trained to handle statutory inspections.
- Use an external company to conduct inspections for you to ensure you are compliant and to get staff used to dealing with inspections. We have an online audit tool that covers all the key questions with a corrective action plan to assist you.
- Ensure you due diligence paperwork is up to date.
- Ensure all your staff are trained on what is expected of them.
- Have clearly marked, easy to use systems for record keeping.
- Know what is expected of you in each of the statutory areas.
- Always incident report an inspection by a statutory authority – make a point of noting any comments they make.
- Have a good working relationship with the authorities – your attitude should be professional, courteous, and helpful at all times.

Who Carries out Inspections?

Enforcing authorities such as the Local Authority, Fire officer, and Police Licensing may visit from time to time to carry out inspections and check compliance with legislation.

In addition, you may also be visited by an appointed insurance engineer to undertake a periodic examination of equipment such as pressurised vessels or passenger lifts as required by specific regulations.

Inspecting Agency	Remit
Police Licensing Unit	Enforcement of the Licensing Act 2003 and criminal laws
Council Licensing Unit	Enforcement of the Licensing Act 2003
Environmental Health Practitioner (EHP) formally referred to as Environmental Health Officers (EHO)	Enforcement of 852/2004 on the Food Hygiene of Foodstuffs. They are also concerned with Health and Safety and environmental health such as Noise.
Health and Safety Executive	Enforcement of the Health and Safety at Work Legislation
Trading Standards	The Consumer Protection from Unfair Trading Regulations 2008
Fire Authorities	Enforcement of fire safety provisions in designated places of work under Regulatory Reform (Fire Safety) Order 2005
HM Revenue Customs	Finance Act (FA) 1994

Since this book focuses on The Licensing Act 2003, we will focus on that area.

A Police Licensing Unit Inspection

They can inspect the whole premises looking for any breaches being made to your premises licence or for any offences being committed (serving to underage persons, serving to drunks, serving outside permitted hours, or any criminal offence being committed).

When they enter the premises, they will produce a warrant card either to the doorman or manager to state who they are and why they are conducting a visit.

Their questions will relate to alcohol, your premises licence, and the four licensing objectives, in particular, the Prevention of Crime and Disorder.

A Council Licensing Unit Inspection

They will inspect the whole premises looking for any breaches being made to your premises licence or for any offences being committed, in particular, overcrowding, public safety, and licensable activities you are providing.

When they enter the premises, they will produce an ID card either to the doorman or manager to state who they are and why they are conducting a visit.

Their questions will relate to public safety (capacities, fire escapes, and equipment), entertainment provided, your premises licence, the licensing objectives (specifically, Public Nuisance, Public Safety & Protection of Children), and they may touch on Prevention of Crime & Disorder (whether you conduct random searching and how you record any crime/report incidents).

Questions You Could Be Asked – Be Sure You Can Answer All of These

1. Who is the Designated Premises Supervisor (DPS)? Are they on duty?
2. Do you have a personal licence holder on site?
3. Can I see your personal licence?
4. Where is your summary of the premises licence displayed?
5. Can I see the full premises licence?
6. What is your total capacity?
7. Before entering, they will usually ask the door supervisor how many people are on the premises
8. Until what time do you serve alcohol and food?
9. Are you aware of the licensing objectives?
10. Do you have a procedure for age checks? Are staff aware of procedures?
11. Are members of staff aware of licensing laws?
12. What staff training have you received?
13. Can I see a record of staff training?
14. How do you report/log incidents?
15. Can we see and check your CCTV system?
16. What are your entry and search policies?

Be sure your team are equipped with clear and concise answers and can locate what they need with ease.

You should also be aware of the following points
- You will receive more visits if you have more incidents.

STAYING OPEN

- Most statutory authorities prioritise inspections on a risk-based system – larger, busier, late licensed premises will receive more visits.

CONCLUSION

You have reached the end of our book – we hope that you have enjoyed it and found it useful.

Compliance is not a destination, but an ongoing journey; best practice and even legislation will change. You will face new challenges as society evolves and times change – never more so than now with the challenges COVID-19 has presented to the hospitality industry.

BETTER Compliance is a mindset and attitude as much as a goal. Approaching legislation and operations with a problem-solving, can-do attitude.

It is no coincidence that the most compliant businesses we work with are also the most successful. We often find that adopting the policies and procedures in this book as well as the ethos of BETTER Compliance has further reaching consequences than just improving compliance. Your guests' experience will improve, as will your service, and the perception of your business will be that of utter professionalism. Team confidence will grow and you'll find that staff retention also improves.

If you would like to continue your exploration and discovery of Better Compliance, there are more tools, resources, and up to date best practice at www.bettercompliance.co.uk.

Businesses that subscribe to our service find that they enjoy peace of mind; safe in the knowledge their key asset—their premises licence—is secure.

Sign up today or contact us for a strategy session.

APPENDIX 1
Better Compliance Licensing Heat Map

Licensing Heat Map

Licence Compliance
- Current Premises Licence available
- Premises compliant with conditions
- Managers knowledgeable of conditions
- Staff know their responsibilities under LA2003
- Personal Licence Holders able to produce Licence
- No irresponsible drinks promotions
- Minimum prescribed measures advertised
- Are staff authorised to make alcohol sales
- No threat of review/enforcement action
- No serious incidents

Licences & Signage Displayed
- Premises Licence summary
- Section 57
- CCTV
- ID scanner
- Search policy
- Drugs
- Age verification
- Please leave quietly

Door Supervisors
- Adequate security provision
- Roles & responsibilities clearly defined
- Log completed & correct

Outside Management
- No recent noise complaints
- Outside areas clearly defined
- Queue & smokers supervised
- Customers vetted prior to entry
- Customers searched
- Outside management & dispersal policy

Fire Safety
- Escape routes clearly signed
- Escape routes unobstructed
- Escape doors available & open freely
- Fire extinguisher properly positioned / within test date
- All fire doors closed
- Fire marshals trained
- Emergency lighting working

Record Keeping
- Daily safety checks
- Occupancy numbers
- Incident reporting policy & incident recorded
- Refusals of entry
- Ejections
- Toilets checks
- Staff training

Internal Management
- Responsible alcohol sales training
- Drugs awareness training
- Staff age verification training
- Staff issued with radios
- Cloakroom available
- First aiders
- Toilet attendant
- H&S policy / risk assessments

CCTV, Body Worn Cameras & ID Scanning Equipment
- Adequate CCTV coverage
- CCTV working correctly
- Staff trained to operate CCTV
- Procedure & record of CCTV checks
- ID scanner used
- Body Worn Cameras used
- GDPR compliant

Policies & Procedures
- Entry controls
- Age verification
- Search / seizure
- Preventing & dealing with intoxication
- Guest welfare
- Drugs
- Ejections
- Security roles & responsibilities
- Prevention & Intervention
- Dealing with serious incidents
- Sexual assaults
- Crime scene preservation
- Theft prevention
- CCTV

APPENDIX 2
Preventing Positional Asphyxiation

Keep your Guests, Staff & Premises
Licence Safe

In light of the tragic and unnecessary death of George Floyd in Minneapolis in May 2020, we have decided to add this chapter to our book.

The purpose of this chapter is to ensure that managers recognise the heightened risk of positional asphyxia during restraint and are alert to the immediate emergency actions to be taken. Positional Asphyxiation is not just something that happens in American law enforcement, all forms of security should be aware of this and trained to prevent it from occurring.

As the manager, you are ultimately responsible for your teams' actions, which include contracted security. You need to be aware of Positional Asphyxia and what you must do to prevent it from occurring.

There are techniques of restraint that have been associated with sudden, unexpected deaths. These are people who die suddenly during restraint by security staff, police officers, correction officers and health care staff.

All personnel must be aware of the potential dangers and take every precaution to ensure they adopt safe practice.

Definition

Positional Asphyxia (also known as restraint asphyxia) can be defined as obstruction of breathing because of restraint technique. It occurs when a person is placed in a posture that prevents or impedes the mechanism of normal breathing.

If the person cannot escape from the position, death may occur very rapidly if this is not recognised.

Death can occur from asphyxia or suffocation. Its important note that any body position that interferes with breathing can cause death.

Background

Research has suggested that restraining a person in a face down position is likely to cause greater restriction of breathing than restraining a person face up. Many law enforcement and health personnel are now taught to avoid restraining people face down or to do so only for a very short period of time. You need to follow suit.

Furthermore, research measuring the effect of restraint positions on lung function suggests that restraint which involves bending the restrained person or placing body weight on them has more effect on their breathing than face down positioning alone.

Risk Factors Which May Increase the Chance of Death

- Kneeling or otherwise placing weight on the subject particularly on the abdomen
- Prolonged (particularly resisted) restraint
- Prior cardiac or respiratory problems
- A person is intoxicated with alcohol or drugs
- A person is substantially overweight (though thin people cannot breathe either if in the wrong position)
- A person is suffering from respiratory muscle fatigue (exhaustion)
- There is some form of airway obstruction
- A person is unconscious for whatever other reason
- Other issues in the way the subject is restrained can also increase the risk of death, for example, any type of restraint holds around the subject's neck

The Downward Spiral

A review of past tragedies reveals a 'downward spiral' leading to the adverse outcome that is common to these cases.

Stage 1 – Development of an Incident
The individual exhibits irrational, violent, aggressive behaviour and/or paranoia. The person may be unusually physically active and aroused. The behaviour causes concern and comes to the attention of a Security Guard.

Stage 2 – Intervention
Attempts at calm rational intervention fail and the decision is made to

physically restrain the individual. A struggle ensues in which the person seems to have unusual energy, requiring several people to restrain them and place them in a prone position. One or more guards are tempted to sit or lean on the subject to maintain control.

The subject may perceive this hostile and fight even harder in an attempt to get relief.

The person may also be fighting harder because they cannot breathe and what is perceived to be increasing violence may actually be increasing desperation to stay alive.

Stage 3 – Exhaustion
The continuing panic and desperation to breathe may cause staff to see the person as a continued threat and apply even more force to restrain them. While struggling with security staff the person expends large amounts of energy trying to breathe. The individual becomes exhausted with low blood oxygen and when they are finally unable to struggle any more, it may be too late.

Recognising the Symptoms and Signs
The first step in prevention is to recognise the risks. This will not eliminate the need to physically control some persons during violent or dangerous incidents but recognising the signs of danger and taking appropriate preventative action may help to reduce the occurrence of bad outcomes.

Managers should pay close attention to the following:
- A person telling you he/she cannot breathe (it should be noted that a person suffering breathing difficulties may not be able to complain about their crisis)
- Gurgling/gasping sounds indicating blockage of the airway and or with foam or mucus coming from the nose or mouth.
- A person shows any visual sign that they are struggling to breathe
- Lips, hands, face discoloured blue due to lack of oxygen (cyanosis)
- Increasing escalated panic, aggression, and prolonged resistance
- Sudden tranquillity – an active, loud, threatening, violent, abusive person suddenly becoming quiet and tranquil, not moving

- A person who displays a heightened level of aggression during restraint may be a physiological response to fighting for air. Any increased resistance during restraint of a person should be regarded with caution.
- A person presents swelling, redness or blood spots to the face or neck
- A person suffers a loss or a reduced level of consciousness.

Standard Operating Procedure

Security staff must recognise the risk of positional asphyxia occurring in the following circumstances and be prepared to respond to a medical emergency:

When a person is:
- Restrained
- Physically ejected
- Left in any position that impedes their ability to breathe normally.

Your team must take the following actions to reduce the risk of positional asphyxia occurring:
- Do not sit or lean or lean on the abdomen ever.
- Once restrained a person should be raised to their feet to a seated or standing position that does not impede the mechanism of normal breathing.
- Avoid prone restraint unless absolutely necessary.
- Care should be taken not to put pressure on the back as breathing can be restricted even if the person is placed in the recovery position.
- Monitoring the person's condition continually whilst being restrained, as death can occur suddenly and develop beyond the point of viable resuscitation within seconds rather than minutes.
- Whenever possible during team restraint, a 'Safety Officer' or 'First aider' is to be identified with the responsibility to monitor the health and welfare of the person during restraint.
- Alert police, if attendance, if restraint has been used on the person.
- Identify persons of increased risk.
- Restraint must occur in direct CCTV sight.
- Ideally this action takes place in the identified 'Restraint Area' which must be covered by CCTV

Staff must take the following emergency actions if positional asphyxia is suspected:
- Call for immediate emergency medical assistance if there is any reason for concern about a person's condition.
- Remove all methods of restraint.
- Place the person in a position that does not impede their breathing.
- If consciousness is lost, check airway and breathing.
- Commence CPR if necessary, but be aware that the oxygen supply in the blood is most likely exhausted by this stage.
- A full record must be made of events a soon as reasonably practical.
- Notify your senior manager immediately.

USEFUL LINKS

Better Compliance
Online licensing compliance system and resource centre
www.bettercompliance.co.uk

RASPFLO
Online staff licensing training – Responsible Alcohol Service and Promoting the Four Licensing Objectives
www.raspflo.co.uk

WAVE
The Metropolitan Police's Welfare and Vulnerability Engagement (WAVE) training
www.nbcc.police.uk/guidance/wave-presentation

Alcohol Licensing
Information on the different types of alcohol licences available and guidance on how to apply for them
www.gov.uk/guidance/alcohol-licensing

Security Industry Authority (SIA)
Information on door supervisors and private security
www.sia.homeoffice.gov.uk

Information Commissioner's Office (ICO)
Information on data protection
www.ico.org.uk

Drink Aware
Information on alcohol
www.drinkaware.co.uk

Talk to Frank
Honest information about drugs
www.talktofrank.com

Ask for Angela
Campaign to keep people safe from sexual assault
www.met.police.uk/AskforAngela

Printed by Amazon Italia Logistica S.r.l.
Torrazza Piemonte (TO), Italy